Create an Atmosphere of Tranquility with an Indoor Zen Garden DIY Guide

Tiarna .U Wilks

Funny helpful tips:

The world is a canvas of endless possibilities; paint your life with bold strokes and vibrant colors.

Embrace change; it's the only constant, and adaptability is a strength.

Create an Atmosphere of Tranquility with an Indoor Zen Garden DIY Guide : Transform Your Home into a Soothing Oasis with Step-by-Step Indoor Zen Garden Building Techniques

Life advices:

Stay committed to quality; it builds brand reputation and customer loyalty.

Practice regular check-ins; they ensure both partners are on the same page.

Introduction

This is a comprehensive guide designed to introduce individuals to the concept, design, and creation of a Zen garden. It provides a detailed exploration of the history, philosophy, and aesthetics associated with Zen gardens, as well as their modern-day significance and use.

The guide begins by elucidating the origins and historical development of Zen gardens, tracing their roots in ancient Japanese and Chinese traditions. It delves into the philosophical underpinnings of Zen gardens, emphasizing their spiritual significance and the principles of mindfulness, simplicity, and harmony that they embody.

The section on Zen garden design explores both traditional and contemporary design approaches, providing insights into the key elements and features that contribute to the overall aesthetic and ambience of a Zen garden. It offers valuable design considerations, emphasizing the importance of balance, proportion, and spatial arrangement in creating a tranquil and harmonious outdoor space.

The guide further delves into the fundamental elements of a Zen garden, highlighting the essential building blocks such as sand/gravel, rocks/stone, plants, and water. It provides practical advice on selecting and incorporating these elements to create a visually appealing and serene environment.

Readers are then guided through the process of planning their Zen garden, including aspects such as location, size, shape, and design. The guide offers suggestions on how to make informed decisions about these elements to ensure the successful creation of a Zen garden that aligns with personal preferences and available space.

Subsequently, the guide provides step-by-step instructions on building a Zen garden, outlining the tools required and the process of preparing the designated space, laying landscape fabric, placing rocks, adding water features, planting vegetation, and adding finishing touches with gravel. It also offers advice on how to nurture and maintain the garden for long-term enjoyment.

Finally, the guide discusses the various ways to enjoy and utilize a Zen garden, as well as common challenges that may arise during its maintenance. It provides practical tips for acknowledging and addressing these challenges while fostering a meaningful and harmonious relationship with the Zen garden.

Contents

CHAPTER ONE

WHAT IS A ZEN GARDEN?

This chapter introduces the historical background and philosophy of Zen gardens, preparing you to learn about their design and elements. By exploring the aesthetic principles of Zen gardens and comparing them to other types of Japanese gardens, you will discover their purpose and significance, investigate their connection to Zen practice, and learn how you can integrate Zen practice while creating your own garden. Finally, we'll look at the significance of Zen gardens today, as well as touch on a few contemporary garden artists to inspire you in the beginning of your gardening journey.

History

During the 14th century, thousands of miles away from the flourishing Renaissance, an equally radical era was beginning in Japan. Fed by the new development of Zen Buddhism, the Muromachi period (named after the district of Kyoto where the shogun's government was located) was a time of great artistic emergence and expansion. The many art forms that began to develop at this time included the tea ceremony, calligraphy, sumi-e ink brush painting, Nōh dance-drama theater, and Zen gardening. In Japan, garden making was—and remains—an exceptional art form considered as significant as calligraphy. By understanding the context in which Zen gardening prospered, as well as its intimate connection with spirituality, you will be prepared to create authentic gardens firmly rooted in history.

Different branches of Buddhism started trickling into the Japanese isles in the sixth century (501–600). Although it originated in China, Buddhism fluidly adapted to Japanese culture, taking on a fully Japanese identity over the course of centuries. In time, Buddhism also found resonance with Shinto, Japan's indigenous religion, practiced on the islands for more than a millennium.

Shinto is an animistic religion, meaning it venerates nature. It is rooted in the idea that everything that populates the earth—from living beings to inanimate objects—is inhabited by a deity. Where Buddhism asks its practitioners to reflect on the transience of life, Shinto invites a reverence toward every aspect of the natural world. In this light, if you see each rock as containing a spirit, you may better understand the sacredness of the Zen garden. Rather than replacing Shinto, Buddhism was adopted alongside it, so that both religions would come to establish the foundation of Japan's cultural identity. Within this environment, the practice of Zen, and the emergence of its notorious gardens, took place.

Zen Buddhism arrived from China as Ch'an Buddhism, Ch'an being the Chinese word for "meditative absorption." It became widely popular in Japan during the Muromachi period (1336–1573) and, interpreted from the Chinese as Zen, began to adopt a Japanese identity. Zen in its new form blended both secular and religious elements. Rather than being considered a religion or even a philosophy, Zen was a practice or, better yet, a way of being. To practice Zen was to let go of all expectations, delusions, and preconceived notions of reality in order to fully surrender to the present moment. At that time, this way of being was revolutionary, and its spirit permeates the gardens built then.

When comparing Zen gardens with those that preceded them, the differences are clear. Pure Land gardens, popular before Zen emerged, were designed to replicate the lush paradise of Amida Buddha, the principal deity of Pure Land Buddhism. In these luxurious gardens, you could observe the changing colors of the seasons, witnessing the ephemeral beauty of the natural world encapsulated in a defined space. Typically used for leisure and recreation, these "pleasure gardens" were created with the intention of giving humans a taste of heaven in the earthly realm.

As Zen gardens emerged throughout the country, austere rocks replaced lush vegetation. Often accompanying Zen temples, these gardens were not meant to be walked through nor nonchalantly gazed at in search of beauty. Rather, Zen gardens were utilitarian; they were used to aid in meditation. While the Pure Land gardens' flora sought to represent the fleeting passage of time, the stones of the Zen garden represented the absolute, unchanging nature of reality. The sternness of the rocks was meant to inspire a feeling of immovable commitment to Zen practice. These gardens condensed nature to its bare minimum, to its very essence. Through watching arid seas of gravel, the viewer was to contemplate the meaning of life. Just as these Zen gardens were stripped of anything unnecessary to reflect nature's true essence, so were its viewers asked to release the superfluous and to embody who they truly were beyond their thinking minds. These enigmatic landscapes helped viewers understand that they were not separate or fundamentally different from the natural world around them.

Among the known early Zen garden designers, Musō Soseki (1275 CE–1351 CE) is by far the most famous. Often called "the father of Zen gardening," he was a Zen monk, groundbreaking gardener, and one of the first in a long tradition of stone-setting priests called Ishi-tate. Soseki created some of the first Zen gardens, most notably those accompanying the temple of Saihō-ji in Kyoto. Originally a Pure Land garden, Saihō-ji's garden later became notorious for incorporating the first dry landscape (rock garden), known as karensansui, in the Zen style. Other Zen monks throughout history also designed gardens, and some noblemen even tried their hand at designing. Although we know some of the creators by name, many Zen gardens were created anonymously. This anonymity is believed to be attributed to the low social status of some of their designers, including laborers. These marginalized workers, unbound by the rules of a social structure that rejected them, were unafraid to experiment with untraditional gardening concepts and innovative ideas, thus heightening the art to a new level.

These revolutionary gardens blazed a trail of equally groundbreaking design ideas still used in Japanese design today. One of the most prominent of these enduring design ideas is the concept of mu, a Japanese character that translates to "emptiness" or "nothingness." An important concept in Zen Buddhism, this spiritual idea, embodied in the use of empty space in a garden, is most starkly realized in the garden of Ryōan-ji temple, which we will further explore later.

Devoid of plants, this rectangular garden is notorious for its lack of attributes and features. The only features of this fascinating garden are 15 rocks and a flat desert of gravel. By reducing the garden to its very essence, every element becomes even more important, with the space between the elements just as vital as the elements themselves.

JAPANESE GARDENS

Japan has a long history of garden design that goes well beyond that of Zen gardens. Together, we'll explore some of the most notable types, from those meant for strolling to a teahouse to study and courtyard spaces.

Shinden and Pure Land Gardens

Shinden gardens and Pure Land gardens emerged during the Heian period (794–1185). They were luxurious gardens that were created and owned by the aristocracy. Lavishly designed, these gardens attempted to reflect the fleeting beauty of the natural world. Large ponds filled with colorful koi and islands connected by arched bridges were notable features of these dreamlike landscapes. Although similar in style, Shinden and Pure Land gardens were created with very different intentions. Shinden gardens lent themselves to leisure and recreation; Pure Land gardens were largely religious in purpose. They were designed not only to honor Amida Buddha but also to give a taste of paradise to their earthbound patrons.

Tea Gardens

While also used to host visitors, tea gardens differed from Shinden gardens in their utilitarian nature. They aimed to prepare teahouse visitors for tea ceremonies. Walking along the stone-paved paths lit up by rustic stone lanterns, guests could surrender to the natural beauty surrounding them and forget about the busyness of the outside world. Extensively adorned with moss, these gardens also commonly featured gates, shelters, and water basins called tsukubai, which were used for ritualistic washing before ceremonies.

Strolling Gardens

Strolling gardens, while also prominently featuring stone paths, resembled Shinden gardens in their extravagance. Designed by feudal lords called daimyo, they often encircled a pond or lake. Visitors could enjoy peaceful promenades along their banks. Some notable attributes of these gardens were practical and ornamental bridges, including stone, arched, and zigzag designs.

Study Gardens

Where Shinden gardens, tea gardens, and strolling gardens were best experienced by immersion, study gardens were meant to be enjoyed from a single point of view, similarly to how you might enjoy a painting. They featured many stone elements such as lanterns, pagodas, and statues. Although Buddha sculptures are popular in Eastern-inspired Western gardens, they were very sparsely used in Japanese gardens and appeared only in those connected to a temple or museum.

Courtyard Gardens

Courtyard gardens, also known as tsuboniwa, may be especially relevant and inspiring if you are working with a smaller space when creating your own Zen garden. Tsubo translates to "two tatami mats" and hints at the size of these tiny plots. These urban gardens were often located between buildings. In addition to providing city dwellers with a hint of nature, they also helped regulate airflow and temperature. Water elements proved to be especially useful in controlling heat. One such feature is the bamboo shishi odoshi, a water feature that uses gravity to release water at intervals, producing a delightful woodsy sound. This feature will be described in more detail in later chapters. Because of their limited dimensions, these gardens were usually meant not to be entered but rather to be enjoyed from outside their boundaries, much like study gardens.

Dry Gardens

Although karensansui are unmatched in their austere appearance thanks to their expanses of dry gravel, rock, and stone, many have traditionally shared several design elements with the gardens mentioned previously. They are unique in their practicality, however. Other Japanese gardens may have offered their viewer a contemplative experience, but no other type of garden served the primary purpose of assisting monks in their rigorous meditation practice. At their heart, Zen rock gardens embody unparalleled elements of vigor and discipline.

Philosophy and Aesthetics

To understand the enigmatic design of Zen gardens, we should first learn about the practice of Zen as it exists in Japanese monasteries. In a monastery, the practice of Zen is threefold: The student practices zazen (seated meditation), samu (work meditation), and chanting. These practices all serve to unify the body and the mind in a state of intense concentration called samadhi, as well as to support the entire monastic community through the individual's dedicated and hard work. It is often believed that samadhi is cultivated only during seated meditation. It is, however, just as important to realize this state while cooking, gardening, or scrubbing the toilet as it is during seated practice. In the planning and maintenance of your own Zen garden, you can bring yourself fully into this state of samadhi and therefore be fully present, giving the best of yourself to your garden. If you practice being completely present in your task, you are practicing Zen. But how exactly do you do it in a practical, everyday way?

ZEN PHILOSOPHY

You practice Zen when you let go of your thoughts and simply follow your breath. In the context of Zen gardening, it may mean consciously removing weeds from your garden one by one, noticing the colors and texture of the weed you are pulling, and observing how the breeze makes them sway from side to side, all the while watching your breath and giving your full attention to this activity. Although this is fundamentally a simple task, it can be quite challenging to do in our world, where we are constantly bombarded with stimuli and digital distractions. But don't be discouraged. The purpose of this meditation is not to "succeed" in clearing your mind. Rather, it is to bring your focus back to the breath, again and again, and to give yourself fully to the moment by offering it your full attention. Your best effort in that moment, your commitment to bringing your attention repeatedly back to the breath and to the activity, whether you are sleepy or angry or distracted—that is the right way to practice Zen and to bring to your garden creation, nurturing, and tending in turn.

When you train your mind in this way, you can more fully appreciate life as it is rather than how you think it should be. Even having small expectations (like those regarding how your garden should turn out) can keep you from enjoying your garden as it actually is. When you practice Zen, you practice having a clear focus, so your mind is fully present in each moment of your life. You can release those thoughts and memories that hurt you or that keep you from fully being yourself. In this state, neither trauma from your past nor fear of the future colors the present. You live each moment perfectly: spontaneously, joyfully, and embodying who you truly are at your core rather than who you were conditioned to be. This immaculate quality of mind can be accessed any time simply by bringing your full attention to the present moment. If you refine your mind in such a way, creativity will flow from you consistently and naturally, resulting in an even more harmonious and authentic garden.

ZEN AESTHETICS

In his book Zen and the Fine Arts, the scholar and philosopher Shin'ichi Hisamatsu explores the seven elements of Zen aesthetics. These characteristics define the aesthetics of Zen gardens, and having a basic understanding of them will help you create your garden. Exploring how a garden can embody these characteristics will also illuminate the practice of samadhi in the cultivation of your own garden. These seven principles are

- asymmetry (fukinsei)
- simplicity (kanso)
- austere sublimity (kokō)
- naturalness (shizen)

- subtle profundity (yūgen)
- freedom from attachment (datsuzoku)
- tranquility (seijaku)

   We'll further explore these principles in chapter 2, but for now, let's look at how a few of them apply to a garden such as Ryōan-ji (see here for an illustration of this garden to help you envision it as you read). The 15 rocks placed on the ground of the rock garden are arranged asymmetrically (fukinsei), and they are deliberately placed so that the viewer cannot, from any perspective, view them all at the same time. Kokō, or austere sublimity, refers to an austerity that is devoid of sensuous aspects; to help envision this, think of something so old that its skin and flesh have disappeared, leaving only bones. Present in things that are weathered by time, kokō carries with it a sense of wisdom or maturity.
   When visiting Ryōan-ji, you do not need to know its age to feel the ancient wisdom in its weathered stones. There is nothing artificial or pretentious about Ryōan-ji; it personifies the natural, but no part of it was created by accident. Embodying shizen, or naturalness, it is distinct from what happens by happy accident in nature, yet it is neither forced nor artificial. Shizen also embodies creativity inherent in deliberate activity. Seijaku refers to a feeling of quietude. Without even the sound of the breeze rustling through leaves on trees, the rock garden evokes a feeling of uttermost tranquility, bringing its viewer the calmness necessary to reflect.
   Rock gardens are not that different from your mind during zazen in that all that is unnecessary has been released. Zen gardens symbolize who you are at your very core, past all the superfluous inward chatter. Stripped of the unnecessary, the rock garden asks you to dig into your life without clinging to the limitations of your intellect. Zen gardens can help you look at the fullness and interconnectedness of things. You can look at the rocks themselves, the space that separates them, and their relationship within the

garden environment—just like you can look at yourself, the world you live in, and how you fit into it.

Zen Gardens Today

After centuries of intriguing the public, Zen gardens continue to mystify and fascinate their viewers. In Japan, the most famous rock gardens still attract hundreds of visitors daily. Some consisting almost exclusively of rocks, these gardens have not changed in appearance, even after almost a millennium. In fact, you can visit more than one thousand traditional Zen gardens without leaving the city of Kyoto.

Centuries-long traditions in stone-setting design are hard to break. But even so, new movements have emerged in the craft of Zen gardening in the last one hundred years. One of the most notable artists and scholars who helped change some of the more ingrained traditions in Zen garden design was Mirei Shigemori (1896–1975), who was inspired by, among other things, Western art movements, including Surrealism and Cubism.

Many of Shigemori's ideas sharply deviated from traditional concepts of Zen gardens. Utilizing unusual elements such as cement blocks and pillars instead of naturally occurring organic elements, Shigemori opened Zen landscape design to new, modernized possibilities of expression. Rather than using nondescript rocks for his dry landscapes, Shigemori chose darkly hued, oddly shaped stones that could both represent landscapes and be seen as sculptures on their own. In addition, to make them stand out even more, he laid his rocks vertically instead of horizontally, a practice typically discouraged in traditional Zen garden design. Shigemori's work can be admired at the temple of Tōfuku-ji in southeastern Kyoto, where his modernist work stands out among the more conventional garden landscapes while creating a feeling of harmony within the landscape as a whole. Let Shigemori's approach—that of gracefully blending new ideas with old traditions—inspire you as you design your garden.

Fascination with Zen gardens now extends far beyond the borders of the Japanese islands. More than 300 public Japanese gardens, many featuring Zen layouts, can be found in North America alone. As Zen gardens have emerged all over the world and grown in popularity, their identities have changed, especially in the West. These gardens no longer serve primarily to aid monks in their difficult Zen training, but they continue to evoke a sense of curiosity in their viewers that can be satisfied only through contemplation.

In an increasingly fast-paced world, with more and more of our lives spent in front of screens, the need for quiet reflection and time spent in nature is even more essential. The expectation of constant productivity often demands constant activity, leaving little time for self-care, reflection, and contemplation. When time is sparse and the outdoors seems too far out of reach, Zen gardens can offer you the serenity and tranquility you need to recharge. The garden expects nothing from you; it simply offers you a serene environment in which to explore your self, to simply be.

By partaking in Zen gardening, you mindfully immerse yourself in a craft that despite being hundreds of years old is still relevant today. Zen gardens appeal to the eye of the trained artist just as much as they do to that of the nature lover. Like Shigemori, you can pay tribute to an ancient practice while incorporating contemporary elements into your garden design. The Zen gardens' more recent aesthetic influences from the West break from the stringent traditional design rules of the past and free you to fully explore your creative potential. With fewer rules to adhere to, you have more room to play.

Of the Ishi-tate, the rock-setting Zen monastic priests of the past, only one remains. Shunmyo Masuno is the only contemporary Zen priest to continue this long and almost extinct tradition. Masuno has been commissioned to design gardens in public and private spaces across Asia, Europe, and North America. His commitment to his craft and his love for every small detail of his work are palpable both in his interviews and in the enchanting gardens he creates. Although Masuno is the only plier of his trade, many beautiful Zen gardens have been created all over the world by ordinary people. Most Zen gardens in the United States were designed by people without Masuno's years of training. Nevertheless, these gardens bring joy and tranquility to their visitors. When creating your garden, do not be intimidated by your lack of experience. If you give yourself over to this kind of garden making, and create a space that brings you peace, no matter its shape, you'll have successfully partaken in the Zen experience.

Writing of his overarching design philosophy, Masuno noted that he "always approaches garden making with both fear and affection. He accepts that it cannot be any better than his ability." As you go forward and learn to design and care for your garden, you will discover how to explore this philosophy in your own work. When you can learn to see any perceived limitations as possibilities, you can rejoice in the exciting opportunity of creating your own special and meditative space.

Creating a Zen garden is more than a mere construction process. It is a chance to reconnect with yourself as well as with nature and the world around you. You may simply want to enjoy a peaceful Zen garden to have a place to reflect, but if you allow it to be, every part of the process—from designing your garden to gathering your elements to caring for your plants—can be a meditative experience. Give your garden your best attention and most valiant effort. Even if it's your very first step, wherever you are in your journey of learning about gardening and Zen practice is where you need to be.

CHAPTER TWO

ZEN GARDEN DESIGN

This chapter introduces you to the traditional and contemporary design elements of Zen gardens. First, we will further examine the seven aesthetic principles that drive Zen art, as well as explore how to embody these concepts in the garden. You will learn about their material and symbolic significance, and see how Zen gardening has changed over time, learning about the elements that have remained and those that have changed. To assist in your design journey, you will find three traditional and three contemporary designs to inspire your process, ranging from beginner friendly to more advanced. Finally, you will be introduced to some important design considerations to think about before starting to design your garden.

Traditional Designs

Together, let's reexamine the fundamental principles of Zen aesthetics we touched on in chapter 1, considering how each materializes in different types of traditional Zen gardens so that you may implement them in your own. These principles were coined centuries after the creation of some of the first Zen gardens; considering that, creators did not use them as exact guidelines when designing their gardens. Even so, they poignantly describe the most important aesthetic elements of Zen gardens.

Many specific design iconographies, some of which even predate the arrival of Zen in Japan, are favored in Zen gardens, and we will explore some of these when looking at the sample designs of traditional gardens. Your garden, however, will more likely feel akin to an authentic Zen garden if you understand and implement the principles that follow into your own individual and unique garden design and planning, rather than if you merely replicate traditional iconographies from other locations different from your own.

A NOTE ABOUT DESIGN ICONOGRAPHIES

Traditional Zen garden design elements follow a set of strict guidelines when it comes to their placement and composition. Some of the most popular features include light-colored gravel or sand raked into patterns, stone compositions, and islands. Examples (which you will find in more detail in the design samples later) include the sanzonseki, or stone triad, as well as the turtle and crane islands. For a truly deep dive into the many iconographies of traditional gardens, I suggest consulting the Sakuiteiki, an ancient text that provides foundation information for creating a traditional Zen garden (see Resources).

ASYMMETRY (FUKINSEI)

This principle is the opposite of what is often embodied in traditional Western gardens, where pruned bushes perfectly mirror one another. Where Western art often searches for perfection, Japanese art deliberately seeks to move away from it. Rather than being chaotic, this lack of symmetry can be dynamic, and it can be used to access a sense of balance and harmony in your arrangements. By not making your garden symmetrical, you free yourself from the formality that's often imposed on nature. Although you should strive to instill this concept throughout the whole design of your garden, you can look at it in more detail in your rock placement and how you mindfully choose different, complementary rocks (we'll explore this more deeply in chapter 3).

SIMPLICITY (KANSO)

By liberating your garden from clutter, kanso gives your space a sense of freedom. You can follow this concept in a variety of ways. The first is to always make sure there are more horizontal lines (features that run along the ground or horizon) in your composition than vertical ones (features that extend upward or toward the sky), allowing you to look at the space between your elements just as much as—if not more than—the elements themselves. Additionally, you can be more conscious in your selection of elements, keeping you from compulsively adding unessential ones.

SUBLIME AUSTERITY (KOKŌ)

This principle reflects a wisdom that can be attained only through age. Whether ancient or contemporary, Zen gardens that follow this concept look timeless, as if they could have been there for a thousand years. Choosing weathered stones and material when assembling your garden, and making sure that all of your elements look stable and anchored, is a key way to explore this concept. Following this principle, your garden should embody an aged maturity and stay away from the fleeting and ephemeral sensuousness of nature; therefore, planting evergreens is preferable to planting flowery, seasonal plants that will need to be replaced and replanted time and time again.

NATURALNESS (SHIZEN)

The name of this concept can be misleading, as it does not refer to the incidental quality of elements typically found in the wilderness. Instead, it refers to the essence of nature. Through careful and intentional design, traditional Zen gardens represent nature stripped of anything excessive or unnecessary. In these gardens, nothing seems manipulated, and yet nothing seems accidental, either. An easy way to approach this concept is by staying away from any element that looks artificial. Avoid painted wood, brightly colored statues, and other kitschy accessories. By following this principle, you respect and trust nature without trying to dominate it.

FREEDOM FROM ATTACHMENT (DATSUZOKU)

By embodying this concept, you let go of all forms of attachment. You let go of your habits, expectations, routines, and adherence to the conventional. Zen gardens are not formulaic. When you follow this concept while making a traditional Zen garden, you can surrender to true creativity. With no expectations, you can fully explore all that your garden has the potential to become. In addition, you can truly appreciate gardening for the art form that it is. You can be creative and give your garden your best effort and energy, but it is a living project: After a certain point, you must let go and watch it flourish on its own.

SUBTLE PROFUNDITY (YŪGEN)

Sometimes also translated as "deep reserve," or "graceful profundity," this concept is difficult to translate to Western thought in only a few words. Yu can translate to "elegant" or "graceful," and gen can translate to "mysterious," "dark," or "profound." The writer Alan Watts has interpreted it as "an awareness of the Universe that triggers emotional responses too deep and powerful for words." An easy way to begin exploring this principle in your Zen garden design is to not reveal everything at once in your composition, but rather to play with subtleties. You can do so by exploring different perspectives; for instance, keep certain elements partly or completely hidden from most points of view.

TRANQUILITY (SEIJAKU)

You can follow this final concept in your gardening by fully focusing your mind on your activity and breath. If your mind is at peace while gardening, this peace will be reflected in the composition and the thriving nature of your garden. To create a calm atmosphere, focus on a muted color palette. Working with shades of green, grey, and beige while staying away from brighter colors will give your garden a sense of quiet calm.

It is important to note that these characteristics are not independent of one another but are interconnected in traditional Zen gardening, as they will be in your garden. Furthermore, you need not always strive for these concepts. Instead, learn to intuitively understand them so that they manifest naturally in your designs and your approach when designing, creating, tending to, and nurturing your garden.

TRADITIONAL DESIGN 1: THE INTRIGUING SIMPLICITY OF RYŌAN-JI

This first design example is one of the most famous Zen gardens in Japan, Kyoto's renowned Ryōan-ji. Let us explore the different design elements of this garden, as well how the most prominent Zen aesthetic principles materialize within it.

The composition of this garden is minimalistic. It is simply made up of rocks, light-grey gravel, and a few patches of moss, with the moss acting as a ground cover on the small islands that host some of the stones. A rectangular garden, it is surrounded by high walls that neatly define the edges of the space, give it a simple backdrop, and keep the sun from giving the light-colored gravel an unpleasant glare.

In Japanese gardens, gravel and sand often symbolize water, but (like all elements of traditional Zen gardens) this representation is deliberately ambiguous to remain up to the viewer's interpretation. At Ryōan-ji, as in many other Zen gardens, the gravel is raked in patterns that further imbue it with a flowing quality.

As with the gravel, the meaning and placement of the stones is ambiguous. There are many theories about what the mysterious setting of these stones could represent, but none are definitive. The 15 rocks are placed asymmetrically, following the concept of fukinsei. This garden features a stone placement arrangement (ishigumi) called the sanzonseki, or "stone triad," a hallmark of many traditional Zen gardens. The stone triad consists of a large rock that acts as a focal point for the composition and two smaller rocks that support this arrangement by adding balance and contrast.

The stones are placed asymmetrically but not randomly. Instead, they are placed so all 15 stones can never be seen at once, demonstrating the intentionality of the design. This intentionality, paired with the uncertain symbolism of the stones' layout, accentuates the subtle profundity (yūgen) quality of this garden. Rather than telling viewers what they are seeing through this design, the garden's creator invites viewers to find a meaning that resonates with them.

The designer of the Ryōan-ji Zen garden did not follow a preset pattern. He did not replicate an existing garden or use a set of defined guidelines to mindlessly set the stones in the ground. This complete creativity imbues his garden with datsuzoku, or freedom from attachment, which permeates the entire design.

THE SIGNIFICANCE OF RAKED PATTERNS

Gravel and sand are often used to symbolize water in Japanese gardens. Like all elements of traditional Zen gardens, however, this representation is deliberately ambiguous to remain up to the viewer's interpretation. This figurative water flows differently depending how it is raked onto the gravel.

Straight lines usually symbolize calm water, while undulating lines represent waves of various sorts. A zigzag pattern can represent a fishnet cast across the sea, and overlapping semicircles may be reminiscent of crashing ocean waves.

One of my favorite patterns is the circle, which can represent a single raindrop hitting the surface of a calm lake. If you have rocks in the middle of your garden, you can use them as a focal point for your raking, progressively raking your way to the edge of your sand garden until the pattern is raked on the full surface. Although in the traditional Zen gardens of Kyoto the pattern is re-raked every day, the patterns in your garden should be re-raked at least every couple of weeks, depending on the weather and other natural disturbances, to look their best.

TRADITIONAL DESIGN 2: THE EVERLASTING STONE RIVER OF DAISEN-IN

Daisen-in is a wonderful contrast to Ryōan-ji. It demonstrates how a Zen garden can display symbolism that is easy to interpret and can be filled with many elements, as long as they are placed mindfully and with intention. In this garden, the influence from Chinese monochrome landscape painting is more visible and obvious than in the other traditional garden samples. The small, L-shaped section of the garden is especially reminiscent of a Chinese ink painting.

The most common interpretation of this garden is one's journey on the "river of life," with many different elements representing this image. On the right side of the garden sits a boat-shaped rock going with the stream, as well as a smaller rock representing a turtle swimming against the current.

In the upper, L-shaped section of the garden, a waterfall of light-colored gravel descends from a rock that represents Mount Horai, a popular and revered iconographic element of Zen gardens. From this waterfall flows a "river of life" represented by the gravel. The river flows all the way to a different section of the garden, where it expands into an ocean.

On the upper-right section of the garden sits, as in the Ryōan-ji garden, the iconographic element of the stone triad, or sanzonseki, a popular stone arrangement (ishigumi) you will see again and again in traditional Zen gardens. Sanzonseki means "the stones of the three saints," and taking its symbolism from Buddhist mythology, this triad originally followed strict geomantic rules. The rocks were arranged on a northeast-southwest diagonal, a path that was believed to be taken by evil spirits, so that the spirits would become trapped and removed by the stones.

Despite looking very different from Ryōan-ji, the same Zen aesthetic principles are shown in this garden. The weathered rocks and mature trees of this composition embody the concept of sublime austerity (kokō). The stone arrangement is deeply reminiscent of stones as you find them in nature while still carrying a sense of human intention, thus representing naturalness (shizen). In addition to sublime austerity and naturalness, this garden displays a deliberate lack of symmetry, embodying fukinsei.

TRADITIONAL DESIGN 3: ONE WITH NATURE AT KONCHI-IN

Kyoto's Konchi-in garden is famous for its exquisite use of many noteworthy traditional Japanese design iconographies. Look at this garden and examine in more detail the concept of shakkei, or "borrowed scenery," as well as the iconographies of turtle island (kame-jima) and crane island (tsuru-jima).

Like the other traditional garden design examples, Konchi-in includes a stone triad (sansonzeki) and raked gravel in patterns reminiscent of water. This garden, however, is best known for its crane and turtle island features. On the left side of the garden sit the head stone and shell stone of the turtle island, while on the right side sit the beak and wing stones of the crane island. These islands, like the stone triads, have origins that predate the flourishing of Zen in Japan. First popularized during the Heian period (794–1185), the turtle and crane islands are an iconic pair. The turtle island (kame-jima) symbolizes stability and longevity, while the crane island (tsuru-jima) represents immortality and the migration of the soul. Together, they exhibit an essential balance in the universe, and so they are always displayed together.

Konchi-in also consists of a large expanse of light-colored gravel that sits closest to the viewer. All other elements are placed at the back of the garden, so that viewer must look past the vast empty sea of gravel to see them. This large, empty space instills tranquility (seijaku) within the composition. The crane and turtle islands, as well as the other rocks and elements, blend harmoniously with their woodsy background.

The ability of the garden to look unified with its background embodies the concept of shakkei or "borrowed scenery." When this concept is followed in creating a Zen space, the garden blends so seamlessly with its surrounding that it looks as if there is no beginning and no end to it, as Konchi-in exquisitely portrays. Through the successful use of shakkei, the principles of naturalness (shizen) and sublime austerity (kokō) illuminate the garden effortlessly. The garden looks completely at home in its space, and there is an aged quality to the composition and the way it interacts with its surroundings.

ZEN GARDEN MATERIALS

Something ethereal lies in the minimal nature of the materials used in traditional Zen gardens, including the following spare—yet essential—elements.

Stones and Rocks

In Shinto, stones were believed to host kami (gods or deities) and were highly respected. This reverence is also present in the traditional art of Zen gardening, which includes many elaborate rules on how to properly set stones. Before the flourishing of Zen gardens in the Muromachi period, rocks were used in Japanese gardens to symbolize meaningful figures, some of which are explored in the design examples. In Zen gardens, this continued practice of rocks symbolizing important figures can be quite ambiguous, as we've seen at Ryōan-ji. In contrast to the gardens that preceded them, Zen gardens are not typically deliberate in their representation of any particular idea, person, or thing; instead, they are meant to inspire the viewer to interpret what they see in the rocks for themselves.

Gravel and Sand

Gravel and sand were revered in Japan before the proliferation of Zen gardens. In the Shinto religion, white and light sand symbolize purity and are used ceremonially around shrines and temples. In Zen gardens, this reverence is still maintained. Gravel is no longer used ceremonially, however; it is often instead used to symbolize water. In some gardens, bridges are even displayed going over "creeks" of small pebbles or gravel. Sometimes patterns are raked upon these bodies of gravel to represent the movement of the figurative water. If water were used instead of the pebbles, then it would simply be itself, and it would not have the ability to represent anything else. Using gravel or pebbles instead of water gives the Zen garden a freedom to be several things—what it is and what it can represent to the viewer.

Evergreens

In stark contrast to the lush vegetation of pleasure gardens, Zen gardens display only a few evergreens. Within Zen gardens, evergreens are meant to evoke a sense of eternity. The Zen garden is not concerned with the purely superficial aspects of nature. Evergreens bring stability amid the passage of time; they are not susceptible to cold or heat and remain unchanged no matter the season.

Combined, these three simple elements (stones, gravel, and evergreens) make up some of the most memorable Zen gardens. They invite their viewers to look for what remains constant despite life's tumultuous changes.

Contemporary Designs

Over the years, Zen garden design has evolved in a multitude of ways. As they traveled outside of Japan, Zen gardens changed to adapt to new environments, locations, and creators. Let's explore how the strict Zen gardens of the past evolved to become today's contemporary Zen gardens.

ADAPTING TO NEW ENVIRONMENTS

The ultimate purpose of a Zen garden is to embody the essence of its environment. Naturalness (shizen) emphasizes this idea: The garden should look at home in its setting. In Japan, the gardens effortlessly accomplish this by echoing their surroundings. They comprise the same granite, moss, and plants that are native to Japan and can be seen everywhere in nature. When you picture a Zen garden, the image of the typical Japanese garden is probably the one that comes to mind. If you understand the purpose of Zen gardens throughout the world, however, it makes sense for them to reflect their environment rather than replicate the specific habitat of Japan.

One remarkable example of this concept put into practice in a climate very different from that of Japan can be seen in California Scenario, an incredible garden designed by Isamu Noguchi, a Japanese American sculptor and artist. The garden, located in the Southern California city of Costa Mesa, is designed to reflect its arid climate. Understanding that the aim of Zen gardens is to embody a microcosm of the environment, Noguchi created a modern garden using contemporary design techniques and completely different elements than those typically seen in a traditional Zen garden in Japan. We'll look at this garden in more detail in one of the examples that follows (here).

FITTING NEW LOCATIONS

On a macro level, Zen gardens adapted to new environments by featuring elements native to their new country or climate, but they also adapted to their new locations on a micro level, such as inside a building, on the roof of a house, or in another atypical and unexpected spot. As the popularity of Zen gardens expanded, more and more private owners became interested in creating them on their own property. As Zen landscapes emerged in private homes, their size and shape changed to fit their new locations. Some contemporary Zen gardens are built inside, while others can be found on patios, balconies, or even on top of buildings, like Shunmyo Masuno's garden ("Seikantei: A Tranquil Haven in Manhattan"). To adapt to these new locations, contemporary designers thoughtfully modified these gardens to fit new perspectives while infusing the essence of Zen aesthetic principles into their spaces.

CHANGES IN SHAPES AND PATTERNS

The shapes and patterns seen within the Zen garden have dramatically evolved over the last century. Influences from Western art movements, such as Surrealism and Cubism, also inspired new and modern concepts in contemporary Zen gardening. The groundbreaking gardens of Mirei Shigemori reflect these artistic influences while still demonstrating a deep reverence and understanding for the art of Zen garden making (for more on Shigemori, see here). Many of his gardens convey this inspiration through his striking juxtaposition of texture, color, and material.

Nebulous shapes of islands, sections with different colors of gravel within the same garden, and eye-catching layering of patterns are among his many contributions to the modernization of Zen gardens.

One of the most notorious examples is the stark yet simple contrast of his checkerboard path stones that slowly fade into moss at the garden of Tōfuku-ji. We'll delve more deeply into some of Shigemori's iconographies later in this chapter.

In addition to these new, innovative patterns, designers also started using rock arrangements to symbolize new themes. While traditional gardens often represented themes inspired by mythology, contemporary designers utilized stones to symbolize patterns meaningful to them. Examples of these new themes include spirals, as designed by the science-inspired designer Shodo Suzuki, and the Big Dipper constellation, as designed by Mirei Shigemori at Tōfuku-ji.

INCORPORATION OF NEW MATERIALS

In addition to innovative and interesting patterns, modern materials like cement and concrete made their way into contemporary Zen gardens. The use of these new materials is illustrated in the Tōfuku-ji temple. When Shigemori was initially asked to design the garden, the temple's priest asked him to make use of extra material that had not been used in a previous temple renovation project, so that the material would not go to waste. With extreme thoughtfulness and consideration, Shigemori used this leftover material to create his breathtaking design.

Not wasting anything is an important concept in Zen; so, if you have unused material of any form or shape from previous landscaping or building projects, explore whether it can be creatively recycled into a section of your Zen garden.

It is worth noting that the designers who dramatically modernized the traditional art of Zen gardening had a thorough understanding (whether innate or acquired) of the purpose and leading principles of Zen garden design. The changes to this art form enriched it, but did not change the purpose or essence of the traditional craft. By respecting these rules and understanding these concepts, they were able to further enhance the art form. By being mindful, you can bring that same understanding into your own designs.

SEIKANTEI: A TRANQUIL HAVEN IN MANHATTAN

This garden, designed by rock-setting priest Shunmyo Masuno, shows how a Zen garden can adapt to a new location and audience. This small, rectangular garden is located on top of a town house in busy Manhattan. It comprises three boulders and a few plants. Tan-colored rocks, slightly larger than gravel, cover a portion of the ground. This straightforward and clutter-free composition embodies simplicity (kanso) in its design.

For this garden, Masuno imported rocks from Japan to add to his landscape. His plants, however, were sourced in New York to ensure they would thrive in that climate. This idea of blending the foreign and the native, the ancient and the contemporary, appears not only in his choice of material but throughout the entire garden. In his composition, Masuno elegantly adapts the art form of Zen gardening to a modern setting, audience, and location.

The two focal points of this garden are its largest boulder and a maple tree, which are both located on the right side of the landscape. The use of perspective and height differences allows the viewer's eye to relax, and the elements' placement intentionally brings about a feeling of tranquility, a trait that gives this garden its name.

Masuno manages to create a garden that resonates with tradition while also introducing contemporary ideas into his landscape. One of these ideas is demonstrated through the unification of the elements outside and inside the garden. He uses the same stone on the side of the garden closest to the viewer as inside the building, making the stone look as if it is going "through" the window. This technique lessens the separation between the viewer and the garden, and seamlessly connects the indoors with the outdoors.

Masuno effortlessly introduces contemporary elements in his garden while still infusing it with the deliberate naturalness (shizen) of a traditional Zen garden. When creating a garden at the request of a private owner, he assumes that the viewer of the garden has a certain understanding of Zen aesthetics. He then thoughtfully selects the traditional elements to keep and the contemporary designs to introduce into this garden. When Masuno has a foreign audience, as in this garden, he makes careful design decisions, understanding that his work acts as a form of cultural exchange.

CALIFORNIA SCENARIO: MODERN MICROCOSM OF THE DESERT

Isamu Noguchi, a Japanese American sculptor and artist, took the craft of Zen gardening and modernized it further. Although he didn't have the same training in Japanese art as Masuno or Shigemori, he created a modern landscape by drawing inspiration from the Zen gardens he visited as a child. Despite its futuristic appearance, this modern design still honors the contemplative quality of a traditional Zen garden.

This garden is a microcosm of its environment in more than one way. Not only does its composition reflect the arid landscape of

Southern California, but its modern design also echoes the urban qualities of its specific location—a plot of land in a city, surrounded by high-rise buildings.

The California Scenario garden is minimal, embodying the concept of simplicity (kanso). Much of it is paved with a warm-beige, golden-colored stone reminiscent of the desert. It features a few boulders that are laid asymmetrically toward the center of the garden. In a bird's-eye view, you can see a large, round island on the upper right of the garden. On this island, several plantings of cacti and succulents (all plants that are native to the region) are displayed.

A man-made water feature flows through the composition from the right side of the Zen garden to the center. The few areas where water flows look almost as if they were painted on the landscape with a brush. Small stones are dispersed in the water, making the futuristic stream more reminiscent of a natural creek.

The stone stream ends at the upper center of the garden, where an imposing blue-grey, pyramid-shaped sculpture dominates the garden's composition. This cool-colored centerpiece vividly contrasts the warm hues of the garden.

California Scenario exemplifies many of the changes Zen gardens have gone through in their modernization, with nontraditional materials and patterns used to ensure the garden reflects its surroundings. In this garden, Noguchi demonstrates a thorough understanding of his environment. He adapted to his surroundings rather than forcing traditional colors, materials, and themes onto this California landscape.

TŌFUKU-JI: TIMELESS MODERNIZATION

The Zen garden at Tōfuku-ji is one of Shigemori's most renowned masterpieces. In this garden, he materializes many modern concepts and ideas, all while demonstrating his understanding and respect for the traditional art form of Zen gardening.

The garden is made up of several sections. One displays iconic checkerboard patterns, with pavers that slowly fade into moss (which we discussed earlier). When he contracted the designer to build this garden, Tōfuku-ji's priest asked Shigemori to reuse some pavers that were left over from a previous building project. Shigemori did not let this material go to waste; he instead used it in a completely innovative display, with a pattern that had never been seen before in a Zen garden.

The grid pattern is used again in a different section of the garden, but this time, Shigemori uses pruned azalea bushes to exhibit this pattern. The geometric checkerboard design is also raked on the gravel, a blunt contrast to the flowy patterns traditionally raked to suggest water.

Another section of the garden also showcases an arrangement using leftover material. Using extraneous foundation stones from a separate building, Shigemori arranged cement blocks in the shape of the Big Dipper, as seen here. In this specific section of the garden, he not only uses innovative, recycled material to create his composition but also explores a contemporary theme through his placement of the rocks.

Traditionally, the placement and significance of stones represented different aspects of Buddhist mythology. At Tōfuku-ji, however, Shigemori placed stones in the form of a constellation, a theme that had never been explored before in Zen gardens. Similarly, you may find that setting stones in a way that symbolizes a motif meaningful to you is a wonderful way to add intention to your garden. In newer interpretations of Zen gardening, symbolism and representation in rock placement are not necessary, but they can be utilized if you decide on something meaningful to you.

In addition to these innovative design elements, this garden is also well-known for the vertical rocks positioned near its entrance gates. Traditionally, rocks chosen for Zen gardens were selected for shapes that resembled a favored animal or element, like the boat at Daisen-in. Despite their resemblance to meaningful figures, those rocks were primarily chosen for their weathered and natural characteristics. In contrast, the rocks adorning the entrance of Tōfuku-ji were purposefully chosen for their striking and eye-catching qualities, in keeping with the garden's more contemporary design style. In this case, the rocks are dark, oddly shaped, and more textured than rocks you would find in a traditional garden.

Design Considerations

There are many considerations to take into account when attempting to create a traditional Zen garden in your location. Let's explore some of these important concepts to understand how to create a harmonious Zen garden based on your location, your environment, and the materials available to you.

YOUR ENVIRONMENT

When you are creating a Zen garden, it is most important to take time to truly examine the circumstances of your specific environment. Perfectly replicating a Zen garden, as you would copy a picture, is usually not a good idea for many reasons. The first is that the garden you have in mind may not "fit" your location. The environment in which you live may have very different conditions than those of Japan. Rocks, plants, and other elements that would look at home and thrive in a Japanese garden may look quite out of place in your part of the world. In addition, if your climate is different than Japan's, it is likely that the majority of Japanese plants you incorporate in your garden would either require a lot more maintenance and resources to survive or would simply perish.

Instead of copying the exact materials and elements of traditional Zen gardens, research plants and rocks native to your region—those that feel like they would suit your space and that seem to have good character. Inspire yourself from the selection process of Shunmyo Masuno, who declared, "When I am looking for suitable stones and other materials for a garden, I go up into the mountains and make numerous sketches in order to find stones and plants with the right degree of empathy." With this same spirit, use intention, focus, and perseverance in your research to find the best elements for your garden, not because they are the same as another garden but because they are the elements best suited to your own unique location.

YOUR LOCATION

Just as traditional Japanese elements may look out of place in your environment, a traditional design may also not be the right fit for your location. If you are working with a nontraditional space—for example, an oddly shaped plot that is covered with concrete—you may need to be creative and flexible to find a design that smoothly integrates with the conditions of your land.

If you attempt to force a design onto a landscape that is not fit for it, the results aren't likely to be harmonious. If, on the other hand, you spend some time really getting acquainted with the strengths and weaknesses of your specific plot, you will find ways for your design to accentuate its best qualities and minimize any shortcomings.

TOO MANY ELEMENTS

When trying to create a perfectly traditional garden, it's easy to get carried away and attempt to incorporate too many elements that you have seen in traditional Zen gardens. You may want to recreate more iconographies than your space can realistically contain.

It may be difficult to be sparse and minimalist in a society where success and happiness are measured by how much you have. This sparse ethos, however, can give your garden a sense of vastness and freedom, no matter its size. As you explore for yourself whether you prefer a more traditional Zen garden or would like to incorporate contemporary elements, be aware that cluttering your garden will take away from its essence. Working with only the original materials —rocks, gravel, and evergreens—is not as limiting as it seems. Within these limitations lie an infinite amount of possibilities for creation!

FREEDOM FROM ATTACHMENT

The previous considerations hint at an essential concept in Zen, which also happens to be a main aesthetic tenet in Zen gardening: freedom from attachment and expectations. This is illuminated in the garden by the creative principle of datsuzoku, or freedom from a routine or formula.

To create a Zen garden, you must be free from expectations of what you originally thought your garden would look like as well as how "traditional" your garden should look. If you have no expectations, you have created room to truly explore what is possible and, more important, what is ideal given your circumstances.

Whether you plan to create a traditional or a contemporary Zen garden, know that you can create a wonderful space no matter your circumstances. If making a traditional Zen garden appeals to you, you can deepen your Zen practice by exploring traditional iconographies and embodying the seven aesthetic principles of Zen art in your garden design, while keeping your design considerations in mind. If a traditionally inspired contemporary garden appeals to you, be mindful of how many elements you bring into your garden (as well as the advantages and limitations of your environment and location); this will enable you to create a thoughtful space. Your attention to detail and repeated focus during your activity will illuminate your design and creation.

Finally, if some of the more stringent traditional rules seem daunting, know that you can still create a beautiful and meaningful Zen garden with a small space, limited budget, and few materials. If you have not worked with plants before or are notorious for forgetting to care for them, know that evergreens tend to be forgiving, and rocks even more so. Through these limits, you can unleash your full creativity using what you now know about the history of Zen, its philosophy, and its aesthetics.

CHAPTER THREE

ELEMENTS OF A ZEN GARDEN

In this chapter, you will learn about the many elements that can appear in a Zen garden. You'll discover different options for sand, gravel, rocks, plants, water features, and additional utilitarian and decorative elements. In each section, you will find important considerations, practical tips, and the average costs for each item you may consider for your design. You will also learn about the significance of each element. After reading this chapter, you will be fully equipped to comfortably choose the elements best suited for your own Zen garden.

Building Blocks of the Zen Garden

As mentioned earlier, the main elements used in Zen gardens are quite simple: Gravel, stone, and a hint of vegetation are all you need to create a harmonious Zen garden. Any other element is supplemental; it is embroidering nature. Keeping this in mind, let's delve into the use, purpose, and significance of each of the essential elements while recognizing that they do not all have to appear in your Zen garden.

Because gravel and stone are the two main elements used, they should be chosen with great care. Gravel traditionally constitutes most of the Zen garden, giving viewers a vast expanse of emptiness to ponder. If you plan to rake patterns in your sand or gravel, select a good quality to avoid unwanted dust particles. For instance, avoid decomposed granite as your gravel because its particles are too fine and inconsistent for raking. Evaluate the size and consistency of the gravel to make sure it is appropriate for your garden. To inform your decision, consider whether you will rake your gravel and the kind of weather to which your garden will be subjected.

Another important consideration is the color of your gravel or sand. You'll find that many types are available in a variety of colors, including different shades of white, beige, and grey. When choosing a color, consider the attributes of the other elements in your garden, particularly the color of your stones. Assess the amount of light and shadow that your garden will receive. Factor in the amount of direct sunlight to which your dry garden will be subjected and whether the sunlight might give your gravel an unpleasant glare, thus disturbing the tranquility of your space. If possible, acquire samples of several different kinds of gravel to see which will best fit your Zen garden.

Likewise, choose your stones (whether used as sculptures, stepping-stones, or another design element) with a great deal of care. Consider how much light and shadow the rocks will receive, and how reflective they may become. You may want to consider how slippery they will get if you are using them as stepping-stones. Stones of different sizes, such as cobblestones and Mexican beach pebbles, can be introduced to add an interesting element to pathways or give texture to islands or other design elements.

Because rocks and gravel usually constitute most of your garden, picking gravel and rocks with complementary colors may be time consuming and require a great deal of care. This task, like that of caring for your garden later, offers an opportunity for you to strengthen your Zen practice by giving yourself over fully to it and focusing your entire attention on the details of the elements you are choosing for your garden.

Once you have selected your gravel and stone, you can start adding plants to your composition. This can present a new challenge, as certain plants have specific requirements for light and shade and will thrive only in specific areas of your garden. Because many plants used in Zen gardens are evergreens, however, they don't require too much care once they've been established. If you're working with potted plants, ensure the soil is moist but not wet, as wet conditions can encourage the roots to rot or the plants to develop a fungus or disease. Many types of shrubs can be pruned into pleasant shapes, such as clouds (which are commonly seen in Japanese gardens), if that is your choice and what creatively excites you.

Water elements, including ponds, waterfalls, and fountains, are less common in traditional Zen gardens. Nevertheless, water features taken from other kinds of Japanese gardens have been used in contemporary Zen gardens, and you may decide to incorporate one in your own space. Although including waterfalls and ponds is ambitious, there is a wide variety of fountains that can add a soothing element and pleasant sounds to your garden, and that will complement traditional and contemporary gardens. Pick a fountain you find aesthetically pleasing and that produces a sound you enjoy. If you buy a fountain online, pay attention to its dimensions and measure out where it will fit in your garden before you purchase it.

Keep purely decorative elements, such as statues, to a minimum. Adding elements such as lights or seating can bring a contemporary ambience to your garden. Light can also accentuate elements already present by steering the eye. We'll discuss additional optional elements, such as bridges, stone lanterns, and bamboo fences, in the last section of this chapter (here).

When choosing elements for your garden, select those that you like on their own. It is equally if not more important to choose complementary elements and to keep the overall composition of your garden in mind. Generally speaking, it is always a good idea to start off with a simple design and few elements and to expand your garden slowly as you become more comfortable. For information on where to find the elements mentioned in the following section, see Resources.

Sand/Gravel

Gravel and sand are essential parts of the karesansui. Gravel often represents water in the traditional Zen garden, with patterns of waves raked onto it. A dry landscape gives the viewer a long, empty expanse upon which to meditate.

Any of the types of gravel we'll explore in the following section will create pleasing patterns when raked. Consider your climate when choosing the sand or gravel that best suits your needs. The smaller the gravel particle, the more easily it will lose the shape you raked into it, or completely blow over, in heavy wind or rain. If you live in an area prone to temperamental weather, opt for larger-grade gravel over sand. If you are working with a larger area, you can save money by purchasing your gravel or sand in bulk, by the yard or ton. If you do so, inquire about delivery costs before you place your order. Buying higher quality gravel and sand will ensure that the size of the particles is consistent and that dust is kept to a minimum.

When deciding where in your yard to place your dry landscape, pick an area away from trees if possible. Fallen leaves, twigs, branches, and other debris can be tedious to collect from your karesansui. In addition to your sand or gravel, you will need a large piece of landscape fabric upon which to lay your gravel. This will keep most weeds from taking over your dry landscape. If your soil is compacted and floods easily, or your climate is prone to heavy rains, you will need to create a simple drainage system underneath the fabric to keep your garden from flooding.

SILICA SAND
$50 to $300 per ton

Silica sand can be used in a dry garden as long as your climate is neither too windy nor too rainy. This is a reliable option if your garden is protected from the elements and you prefer finer particles. This sand consists primarily of quartz and can be found in shades ranging from white to amber. Inquire about the particle size before purchasing. Look for coarse silica sand if available and choose a sand with the particle size no smaller than 0.4 mm (5/32 in.). Being thin, it will lose the shape you rake into it more easily than the other gravels mentioned in this section.

LIMESTONE CHIPPINGS

$28 to $45 per ton

Made of slightly larger particles than silica sand, limestone chippings are a good fit for those seeking a fine material but who are not in a climate where sand is suitable. They are available in a range of colors from white to various shades of grey. They are preferable in sizes ranging from 8 mm to 14 mm (5/16 in. to ⅜ in.) per particle. Being larger and more porous than particles of silica sand, limestone chippings will hold patterns raked into them longer.

POULTRY GRIT

$60 to $100 per ton; $10 per 5-pound bag

Poultry grit is a finely ground substance made of rocks that is commonly fed to chickens and turkeys to help with their digestion. This grit is often refined to the perfect size and consistency for a Zen garden. Poultry grit is easily found by the bag, which is convenient if you are working with a small area. It is a fine alternative to other options and can be easier to source. You are more likely to find this product sold by a farmer than a landscape supplier.

PEA GRAVEL

$3 to $5 per 5-cubic-foot bag; $33 to $50 per cubic yard

If you are not planning to rake shapes into your garden, any gravel with a smooth edge will work. A favorite of many contemporary Zen garden designers, pea gravel is usually readily available. It comes in a variety of different sizes and colors, including white, beige, brown, and grey, varying in price based on its color. Like poultry grit, it is easy to find by the bag, making it good for working with small areas.

CRUSHED GRANITE

$25 to $50 per ton

Crushed granite is the most authentic gravel you can use in your garden, and it is the most common material in Japanese Zen gardens. It may be difficult to find depending upon where you live, however. It is available in a variety of colors, including shades of brown, grey, black, white, blue, green, and red, although you may want to stick with grey, beige, and white for a tranquil, traditional garden. The best particle size for raking ranges from 2 mm (5/64 in.) to 15 mm (about ⅝ in.).

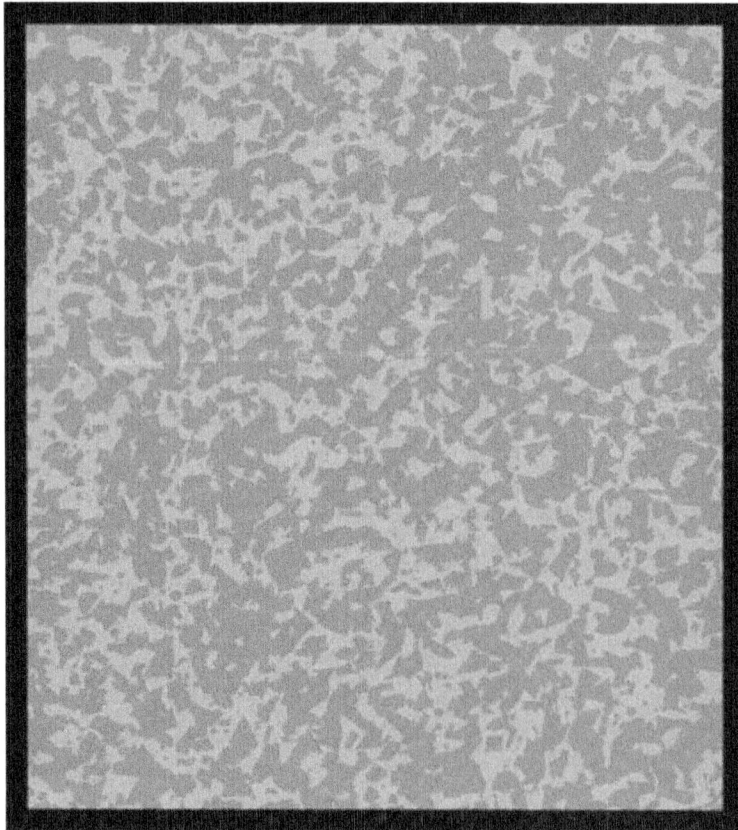

Rocks/Stone

Traditional Zen gardens are among the rare gardens in which rocks often have more importance than plants, so you should select rocks with the utmost attention. In the middle of your dry landscapes, these rocks can act as focal points and attract the eye. They do not, however, need to have a shape that stands out like that of a sculpture; they can simply be rocks that look like rocks.

In a traditional garden, these rocks should look old and weathered. If your climate allows for it, rocks covered with lichen or moss can add a wonderful ancient-looking accent to your Zen landscape. While planting moss onto a rock is difficult, you may be able to find a rock from the wild that already has moss and lichen on it. When inviting the chosen rock into your garden, however, you must make sure that its new conditions are like the ones found in the wild, considering factors like shade and sunlight, humidity, temperature, and cardinal direction. This will give the moss and lichen the best chance to thrive.

Any rocks or boulders you choose should be firmly anchored in the ground so that they look very stable, as if they have been in your garden for years.

If you are creating a contemporary Zen garden, you have more freedom when choosing and placing your rocks; they can be oddly shaped or colorful.

You may find rocks on your property appropriate for your rock garden, or you may find them in a nearby field. Although removing rocks from nature is not usually a problem as long as it does not disturb their ecosystem, always inquire before removing a rock from a property that is not your own. Fieldstones can be a problem to farmers, who are often willing to let go of them for free. Local landscaping companies often carry fieldstones as well. Because these rocks act as sculpture, you should generally not source them from quarries, where they will have recently been crushed and therefore will not embody the weathered quality we seek in our gardens.

Granite is the material of choice in traditional Japanese Zen gardens. If granite is not local to your area, choosing another dark-colored rock, like gneiss or schist, will still bring a traditional touch to your garden. Nonetheless, since the purpose of a Zen garden is to create a microcosm of nature, it is better to choose rocks local to your area rather than to import large stones. Not only will local stones be cheaper, but they are also more likely to fit seamlessly into your garden and to truly capture the essence of your unique local nature.

As with sand and gravel, it is advisable to check for delivery and installment fees before purchasing rocks, especially larger rocks. Prices may vary widely depending on factors such as where the rock is being sourced, the provider, the weight and size of the rock, and the delivery distance.

FIELDSTONES

Anywhere from $100 to $600 per ton

Fieldstones, sometimes called boulders, are great for giving a sculptural element to your garden. They can also make beautiful, authentic pathways if they are mostly buried in the ground, revealing only their flat edges to step on. They are preferable to others since they are naturally occurring rocks in your area and therefore reflect the environment where you live. You can have these rocks delivered from a landscape supplier, or you may find a local farmer willing to part with them for free.

You can bury fieldstones with a flat edge to make a path as is done in the traditional fashion, but note that this does require more labor than using slab. That said, it does not require any special equipment. You can find instructions on how to build these kinds of paths, called tobi-ishi paths, in <u>chap</u><u>ter 5</u> (<u>here</u>).

FLAGSTONE SLAB

$2 to $6 per square foot

If you prefer not to use flat fieldstones to make your pathway, you can create lovely paths with flagstones. Readily acquired from most landscaping suppliers, they will give your pathway an asymmetric, weathered appearance. If you expect your pathway to get a lot of traffic, consider using a durable stone such as limestone or bluestone. If the purpose of your pathway is mainly decorative, choose a stone most complementary to the rest of your garden.

PAVERS

$4 to $6 per square foot

While using uncut flagstone slabs will make your garden more traditional, pavers will bring symmetry and modernity to your garden. Flagstones and pavers can be used together for a contemporary pathway, or pavers can be used on their own. Like flagstones, pavers are available in a wide array of different stones. Opt for a local material that blends with the rest of your garden. For a weathered, calming look, consider granite or bluestone pavers. On the other end of the spectrum, concrete pavers are a cheaper alternative and bring a truly modern appearance to your garden.

COBBLESTONES

$10 to $20 per square foot

Usually made from granite or basalt, cobblestones are a versatile element in the Zen garden. They can be used in many ways, including defining the borders of your sand garden and adding texture to a section of your pathway or island. Along with other smaller rocks, they can be used to create a dry creek. Because cobblestones can be expensive, use them in a decorative rather than utilitarian way, they will add an interesting design element to already existing features.

MEXICAN BEACH PEBBLES

$20 to $30 per bag; $0.35 per lb.

These stunning, rounded rocks can bring a delightful decorative element to your contemporary Zen garden. They can be found in a variety of colors. Like cobblestone, these pebbles can be used to create a dry creek or add an element of interest to your pathway. They also can be stacked in interesting ways to add texture to islands or edges.

OTHER OPTIONS

Similar to Mexican beach pebbles, rainforest river rocks can be found in a multitude of different colors and can add a different element of texture and color to your garden. Although they may be more expensive than other stones, you may find polished exotic pebbles to be a nice addition to your garden, depending upon your budget. Riprap stones, angular stones found in larger particles than gravel, may also be a good option.

As far as bigger elements are concerned, do not be afraid to explore less traditional materials, such as concrete, if you are creating a contemporary Zen garden. Although nontraditional, concrete stones can look harmonious with the rest of your garden if used thoughtfully.

Plants

Plants can provide soothing balance to your space. Emphasis is traditionally placed on evergreens and other plants that are less susceptible to seasonal changes. In addition to evergreens, moss is also featured in many traditional Zen gardens, where it symbolizes age and harmony. The most popular evergreens used in traditional gardens are pines: notably, the Japanese black pine. This pine is traditionally viewed as masculine, and its common counterpart, the red pine, is traditionally viewed as feminine.

These pine trees, along with the other shrubs in the list that follows, can all be found in dwarf forms. A dwarf variety of a plant will grow incredibly slowly and will remain small even at maturity. For these reasons, they make a good fit for smaller gardens on patios or balconies. Whether or not you find them in dwarf forms, the trees and shrubs referenced in this section will grow well in containers. You can keep them in pots or transplant them into the ground when you feel ready. Starting off by keeping your plants in pots will give you the flexibility to move them around later.

Some plants in the list that follows can be pruned into bonsai, which are different from genetically dwarfed trees. A bonsai can be made from most trees; it does not indicate a tree species. Rather, it refers to a set of techniques used on a tree to miniaturize it. Learning to make bonsai out of trees or shrubs is beyond the scope of this book; I encourage you to further research this topic if it is of interest to you (see Resources).

Most plants suggested here are native to Japan and do not require a lot of maintenance under the right conditions. Depending on the zone in which your garden is located, you may have difficulties finding them, or they may not thrive in your climate (for more information on finding your growing zone, consult the sidebar in chapter 4, here). For this reason, I suggest you find similar pines, shrubs, and ground-cover plants native to your region. A professional at a local nursery can recommend local, easy-to-care-for plants that will embellish your garden.

Another simple but extremely effective way to choose plants that will prosper in your garden is to walk around your neighborhood and in nearby parks, and note the trees and plants that you see. This will give you an idea of the plants that are either native or have adapted well to your climate: These plants will more likely thrive in your garden and be simpler to maintain. If you still feel intimidated by working with plants for the first time, remember that evergreens, once established, tend to be very low maintenance and resilient!

MOSS (BRYOPHYTA) AND SIMILAR GROUND COVERS
$5.00 per square foot

Moss makes a wonderful ground cover. It can be used on top of rocks, between stepping-stones, or on islands. A few disturbance-tolerant mosses that you may find easy to grow in your garden are purple moss (ceratodon purpureus) and silver moss (bryum argentum). Every zone has native mosses, so choose a moss native to your region.

When purchasing moss, be conscious to match the preferred conditions for the moss you buy to those in your garden. Furthermore, be aware that although moss in not always easy to propagate at first, once it becomes established, you may have a hard time stopping its growth.

Two ground covers that look similar to moss and may be easier to propagate and grow are Irish moss (sagina subulata) and baby's tears (soleirolia soleirolii). Irish moss is the common name of this ground cover; however, it is not actually moss, but a low-growing evergreen perennial that resembles moss, yet is actually part of the carnation family (Caryophyllaceae).

Most moss thrives in dark and shady conditions, and optimal pH depends on the specific variety. It receives its nutrients from the air rather than soil. Select a location for your moss that is hidden from sun for most of the day. An ideal planting site will be close to a water source. Keep the moss moist for the first three weeks after transplanting it by regularly spraying it with water.

CREEPING THYME (THYMUS PRAECOX)

$10 and up for a 3-inch plant

If the area in your garden that needs ground cover is sunny, creeping thyme is a reliable alternative to moss.

This plant is especially ideal to use between stepping-stones, as it is not sensitive to light foot traffic and will prevent weeds from sprouting. As it is a perennial plant, you won't need to replant creeping thyme every year. It is also deer- and rabbit-resistant, and it is attractive to bees.

Creeping thyme is hardiest in zones 4 through 9. It prefers full sun, well-drained sandy soil, and neutral to slightly alkaline pH, but it is adaptable to different light and soil conditions. The first three weeks after you have planted it, make sure it does not dry out by keeping the soil moist but not wet. After it has been established, creeping thyme will be drought tolerant and require very little to no maintenance. This plant does not like humidity. If you live in a humid environment, add sand to your soil to prevent it from getting too moist. For best results, plant in the spring or fall.

JAPANESE HOLLY (ILEX CRENATA)

$20 and up for a 2.5 quart (7- to 12-inch) potted plant

This low-maintenance shrub is very popular in Zen gardens. Japanese holly is an evergreen with a beautiful dark green foliage. You can use it in your garden as a hedge or as an accent plant.

The Japanese holly grows best in zones 6 through 10. It will thrive in sun or partial shade and prefers a well-drained, acidic soil. Once established, it is resistant to any negative effects from air pollution, making it a good choice for urban environments.

When transplanting your holly, mulch it with pine needles or wood chips to keep its roots moist and cool. Water it in summer and let it dry out in fall to help it better weather the winter. Although not necessary, it does respond very well to pruning. Plant your Japanese holly in early spring and prune it in late winter or the following early spring.

Since this plant grows very slowly—only about an inch per year—it will thrive if grown in a pot. You can also find dwarf Japanese holly. When planting it in a pot, use a 50/50 mix of potting soil and compost and plant it in a pot that has good drainage holes. Inside a container, Japanese holly prefers moist soil. It can successfully be trained as a bonsai as well.

JAPANESE YEW (TAXUS CUSPIDATA)

$20 and up for a 1 gallon (5- to 10-inch) potted plant

Like Japanese holly, Japanese yew is a slow-growing evergreen commonly featured in Zen gardens. Rather than leaves, however, this shrub's needle-like foliage can provide a hedge or an accent piece.

This plant is easy to care for. Once it has been established, it will be tolerant to drought, salt air, and pollution, and it can live for hundreds of years. This plant is poisonous to humans and pets, so be mindful of that fact if selecting it for use in your garden.

It grows best in zones 5 through 9 and is very adaptable to soil and light conditions. It will thrive in full sun, partial shade, and even full shade, and although it prefers moist soil, it will tolerate most well-drained acidic, neutral, or alkaline soil. During the summer, mulch it with shredded bark or pine needles to keep the roots moist and cool. Plant it in early fall or spring and, if you wish, prune from spring to fall.

You can also find Japanese yew in a dwarf form, and it will grow well in a container. Make sure your pot has good drainage holes and keep its soil moist. Like Japanese holly, it can be trained as a bonsai.

JAPANESE BLACK PINE (PINUS THUNBERGII)

$35 and up for a 1 gallon (5- to 15-inch) potted plant

With its irregular branches and darkly hued bark, Japanese black pine can make a wonderful addition to your garden. Although it can be used for hedges or background plantings, it is typically grown as a single design element in traditional Zen gardens. In these gardens, black pines are regarded as masculine and symbolize longevity. They are often found on top of a crane or turtle island.

Black pines are tolerant of salt air, wind, and dry soil, but they are sensitive to air pollution, making them a less than ideal selection for an urban Zen garden. They grow well in zones 5 through 9, and prefer sandy, acidic soil. They also prefer full sun or light shade. During the first year you transplant it, water it weekly in the absence of rain. Apply a complete 10-10-10 granular fertilizer every year or two if the quality of your soil is especially poor. Plant it in spring or early fall.

The Japanese black pine grows well in a container and exists in a dwarf form. In a pot, let the soil dry out completely before you water it. If you keep the container outside, protect the pot from the sun to avoid root burn. If pruned regularly, it is one of the best trees to train as a bonsai.

JAPANESE MAPLE (ACER PALMATUM)

$35 and up for a 1 gallon (5- to 10-inch) potted plant

The Japanese maple has provided inspiration to many artists and poets who have praised its transient beauty. In Japanese gardens, it symbolizes peace and serenity. With its green foliage in the spring and iconic crimson foliage in the fall, it is a favorite of contemporary Zen gardens. These small trees can be used as a single design element to bring a touch of color to balance the rest of your garden.

Japanese maples are hardiest in zones 5 through 9. They thrive in moist, fertile, neutral pH soil and partial shade. Be careful not to plant them in full sun, as their leaves can easily become scorched. If you plant one in the ground, water it regularly for about a year until it is well established. Plant in the spring or the fall when there are no threats of frost.

Japanese maples are "self-stunting," which means they will not grow any taller if their roots cannot expand. For this reason, they will grow especially well in containers with adequate drainage holes. Like the other shrubs and trees on this list, the maple can also be trained as a bonsai.

OTHER OPTIONS

A popular plant in contemporary Zen gardens is bamboo. Many varieties are fast-growing invasive species that can quickly overtake your garden in the right conditions, so choose bamboo mindfully. To mitigate their invasiveness, you can buy a bamboo shield to install at the roots of the plant or use a similar barrier to contain the roots.

Bamboo will grow well in a container and will add a sophisticated and refreshing touch to a small patio or balcony Zen garden.

If you are looking to grow a plant in especially wet conditions, consider growing horsetail. This plant, like bamboo, spreads very easily, so you may want to use soil barriers or grow it in pots. On the other end of the spectrum, if you are looking for plants that will thrive in especially dry climates, consider succulents, which bring a modern touch to your contemporary garden.

The wide array of good alternatives to ground-covering species includes creeping junipers, Mondo grass, and Elijah blue fescue. If black or red pines do not work in your climate, juniper is a great alternative that is also traditionally used in Zen gardens.

Finally, if your garden would benefit from a vine, consider wisteria, which adds a beautiful touch of lavender color to your garden when it blooms in the spring. Like bamboo and horsetail, wisteria can be invasive, so choose it mindfully.

Water

Water plays an essential role in the Japanese garden, where it represents purification and cleansing. Water itself is not always present as a feature of the garden, however. As mentioned previously, Zen gardens typically use sand, gravel, or pebbles to represent water. The rocks fulfill this purpose by being shaped like a running stream to form a dry creek, or by being raked into patterns representing the movement of water. Because of these representations, actual water does not need to appear in a Zen garden to make it complete.

Water fountains, ponds, and waterfalls still commonly appear in traditional and contemporary Zen gardens, however. Since the contemporary purpose of creating a Zen garden in the West is to create a peaceful space in which to relax and contemplate, adding the burble and flow of water can help create a soothing atmosphere in which to relax your mind and to meditate. Even if you are working with a small area, you can add a water element to your garden. Although ponds and waterfalls can be very expensive and laborious projects to undertake, you can still include a water feature in your garden by installing a contemporary or traditional fountain.

The shishi odoshi, a traditional water fountain constructed from bamboo, will fill your garden with both the relaxing melody of water and the woodsy sound of bamboo. Plenty of other elegant modern or traditional fountains are available online and from your local landscape supplier. If you are building a garden on a budget, it is wise to calculate the utility cost of your fountain running in your garden before acquiring it. Most water fountains usually cost less than $50 a month to operate, but this may be different based on your energy provider and the size of your pump.

To properly maintain a fountain, make sure that water levels remain constant, as some water will naturally evaporate. It is healthier for your water pump to run all the time, as it will keep the water cleaner. Using distilled water and changing the water in your fountain regularly will prolong the life of your water pump. Finally, if your garden is in a climate subject to freeze cycles and strong temperature changes, your fountain should be brought indoors if strong heat fluctuations occur to prevent any cracks. Alternatively, drain the water, clean and remove the pump (and store it inside during the winter), and wash the fountain. Once the fountain is empty and clean, you can either buy a fountain cover or enclose your fountain with an absorbing fabric and a secured tarp to protect it from freezing temperatures.

SHISHI ODOSHI

$60 and up; $30 for materials

Originally designed to scare away deer, these bamboo fountains can add a splendid musical element to your garden. They consist of several pieces of bamboo, one of which fills with water. Once it is full, gravity pulls it down to release the water, making a pleasing woodsy sound as the bamboo taps down. These fountains can easily be found online or from a specialized supplier. If you own a drill, however, these fountains are surprisingly easy to make, as they consist only of bamboo, tubing, a basin, and a water pump. See Resources for guidance if you wish to make your own.

CONTEMPORARY WATER FOUNTAIN

$40 and up

Sophisticated, elegant, and modern fountains are readily available from your local supplier or online and can give your garden a touch of harmony and sophistication. For a traditional garden, favor hand-chiseled stone fountains, and for a modern garden, choose a fountain with strong linear qualities. Consider fountains equipped with LED lights for added illumination if you intend to enjoy your garden in the evening. These fountains can vary greatly in price and quality, so do the necessary research before buying one.

TSUKUBAI

$400 and up

A tsukubai is a water basin traditionally used for visitors to purify their hands and mouth before entering a holy place. These granite basins were commonly used before entering a Buddhist temple or attending a tea ceremony. Because of their popularity in tea gardens, they have made their way into contemporary Zen gardens as well. These simple, often unadorned water features can add a traditional element to your garden without visually cluttering it. Tsukubai can be found from stone designers or suppliers that specialize in Japanese-style rock ornaments.

OTHER OPTIONS

If you have the space, time, and resources for them, installing a pond or waterfall can add a serene element to your garden. These types of projects can be expensive, usually costing at least $1,000 per project. Furthermore, they require a fair deal of maintenance, which you need to factor into the overall cost. If you really want to add these features to your garden and don't know where to start, specialized companies make DIY kits that run anywhere from $1,000 to $5,000 for you to construct your own pond or waterfall. These kits contain clear instructions and all the materials necessary for you to start your project with suitable framework and guidance.

Additional Elements

Besides rocks, gravel, and evergreens, any other element you bring to your garden is purely optional. You may decide to add additional elements to serve a utilitarian or decorative purpose, or to make your garden feel cozier and more personal. Some elements, such as benches for sitting or lights to accentuate certain features at night, can be very useful and help bring attention to specific parts of your garden. Having these elements present may make your garden feel more comfortable and invite you to spend more time in it.

Other elements, such as statues and stone lanterns, can be purely decorative. If Japanese garden aesthetics appeal to you, you may enjoy incorporating elements traditionally found in these gardens, such as stone bridges or wooden gates.

Remember, when adding purely decorative elements to your garden, keep the seven principles of Zen aesthetics in mind (here). Use these items sparingly, for having a space free of clutter helps facilitate a mind free of unnecessary thoughts. Keeping decorative elements to a minimum also helps maintain the Zen feeling of the garden. If you are in doubt, add these elements very slowly, one at a time, and do not be afraid to remove them if you feel that your garden is becoming too busy or cluttered.

SEATING

$30 and up

Traditionally, flat rocks were used for the viewers of the Zen garden to sit on and meditate. Nonetheless, you may find sitting on a rock quite uncomfortable and would prefer to find a seating option better suited to your needs. Prioritize your comfort and the simplicity of the seat. Benches and patio chairs are fine options. Before purchasing them, consider whether their color and design will complement the rest of your composition, and avoid flashy colors and designs that will look out of place in your Zen garden. Place your benches or chair in an area of your garden from which you can observe your entire garden, or in a spot that you feel is especially serene and will bring you calm.

AMBIENT LIGHTING

$15 and up

Adding lighting to your garden enables you to enjoy it in the evening and at night. While hanging lights can add a festive element to your space, spotlights can be used to bring attention to specific elements. Popular in contemporary gardens, spotlights are used to accentuate rocks, water features, and pathways. If you are using spotlights, consider the angle at which you place the light. You may try to choose its permanent place in the evening when you can test out different angles to see which one is the most harmonious.

STONE LANTERNS

$100 and up

Stone lanterns, in different shapes and sizes, are popular elements of traditional Japanese gardens. Made of granite, they were traditionally used to light the way for teahouse visitors. They can still be found outside Zen temples around the world. These weathered-looking lanterns can add both a traditional and an ancient-looking element to your garden. Since these lanterns tend to be quite heavy, inquire about delivery and shipping costs before placing your order.

BRIDGES

$80 and up for wood, $500 and up for stone

Even if you do not have a pond or stream in your garden, you may want to include a bridge for its aesthetic purpose. Bridges can add an interesting element to your garden, and they do not have to be utilitarian. In some traditional Japanese gardens, bridges are to be used only by kami, or spirits, and they are therefore decorative. You may pay homage to this tradition by adding a small decorative bridge to your garden. You can also run a bridge over any figurative water feature, whether a dry creek or gravel, for either a kami or a human to use.

OTHER OPTIONS

Other utilitarian options include gates and fences. Bamboo fences can separate different areas of your garden or cover any wall that seems not to fit with the rest of your space. Gates may also be useful to your space. Find inspiration from the style of gates traditionally found at the entrance of tea gardens, which lend a wonderful rustic and weathered quality to your landscape. Other decorative elements, such as statues, can be added to your garden, although they should be chosen with taste and used sparingly to avoid cluttering your Zen space.

CHAPTER FOUR

PLANNING YOUR GARDEN

In this chapter, we explore different important considerations to help you determine the best location, size, and shape for your garden. You will also discover ways to choose elements that will fit into your garden space harmoniously while placing them according to Zen aesthetic principles. Finally, you will find a list of clear and easy steps to follow to start planning your garden. Several design samples are provided, ranging from small, inexpensive, and simple to more advanced, ambitious, and elaborate designs. These samples feature gardens with different uses, styles, and locations so you have a wide array of options to inspire your creative process when it comes to designing your garden.

Location

Depending on your circumstances, deciding where to position your garden could be simple. You may have only a limited amount of land to work from or have access to only a small balcony or patio. Having to create a garden in a little space is an ideal way to learn how to make the best of your limitations. Prepare to be flexible and creative in your decision-making—a nontraditional situation often requires nontraditional solutions. If you plan to place your garden in an area covered in concrete, for example, you can easily lay a piece of landscape fabric on top of it and cover it with gravel. You can adorn this dry landscape exclusively with carefully chosen potted plants. When it comes to transforming a nontraditional space into a wonderful garden, infinite creative solutions are available to you, and you do not need to design a perfectly authentic Zen landscape to create a meditative space that will bring you joy and serenity.

On the other hand, if a larger piece of land is available to you and you have several options from which to choose, determining the ideal area for your garden may be more challenging and require you to consider several factors.

To select the optimal placement of your garden, start off by clearly setting your intentions. Define what you want from your space. Consider, for instance, how you will interact with your garden. Will it be enjoyed visually, from only one or a couple of perspectives? If so, you should consider placing it in a well-lit area, at a distance from which you can enjoy it from your preferred vantage point. Or will your garden be one that you interact with, walk through, and enjoy from within? In this case, you may prefer to situate your garden in a shadier area, where you will be able to appreciate it without being bothered by the sun.

If your garden is to be a visual one, consider the direction that it will face. For example, if you design a garden with the intent of viewing it only from one direction and look forward to meditating in front of it at sunrise, you may reconsider having your garden facing west, as the sun rising in the east may blind you and inhibit you from appreciating and using your garden to its fullest potential.

In addition to these factors, understanding how you will interact with your garden will help you decide whether it is best suited for your front yard, side yard, or backyard. An area that you frequent or look at often will allow you to relish the sight of your garden on a regular basis; therefore, a visual garden may work best in the front yard or the backyard. On the other hand, a garden that is to be interacted with from within is often more intimate. It may fulfill its purpose more successfully in your side yard or backyard, where you can appreciate it with more privacy. You'll also want to consider how accessible your garden should be to you and other visitors. Your preference around the ease (or difficulty) of access to your garden can also help you determine its ideal positioning.

Once you have a general idea of where to locate your garden, observe this location carefully. Pay attention to how many hours of sunlight it receives per day and consider the type of soil you are working with. Notice the quality of drainage in the area: On the next rainy day, pay attention to whether puddles are forming in your chosen space—this is an indication of poor drainage. In addition, consider whether the space contains mature plants that may be difficult to work around or that would need to be transplanted or uprooted. If you already have an idea of the varieties and types of plants you intend to include in your garden, their specific needs will further inform your decision.

Take other considerations into account when deciding where to place your dry landscape. Because a gravel garden requires a flat area, the organic elevation of your landscape can inform which space is best suited for it. Naturally occurring mounds in your yard can become islands in your sea of gravel or form a natural curve delineating the edge of your dry garden. On the other hand, if your yard consists primarily of hills and does not seem suited for a traditional karesansui, do not get discouraged. In place of a sea of gravel, you can create an equally delightful dry creek to run through such hilly mounds. (You will find a sample design for a dry creek garden here).

In addition to considering the natural elevation of your garden, you may want to consider placing your gravel garden away from any trees to avoid debris; as mentioned earlier, this is especially true for deciduous trees, as they drop many leaves. If you plan to rake your garden, avoid areas that you know are heavily trafficked by pets or wildlife. Furthermore, take notice of whether your chosen location is an area that birds like to frequent. If you plan to use a light-colored gravel, bird droppings may dirty it and require more maintenance that you had anticipated.

In addition to these practical matters, get to know your space in order to understand its strengths and shortcomings. Consider your chosen location and ask yourself: What are its limitations? What makes it special? You may decide to place your Zen garden in your favorite part of the yard. If you do so, take notice of what you think makes it special before you alter it with your garden design. You want to make sure you do not change this piece of land in a way that takes away from what you loved so much about it in the first place. Instead of locating your garden in your favorite part of the yard, consider creating a garden in the area that you find least attractive. Rather than enhancing something that you already find beautiful, you can turn an area that you find less favorable into your new favorite part of your property.

Size

To choose the most appropriate size for your garden, start off by realistically examining your options. First, look at how much money you plan to invest in your garden. Then, research the prices of the elements you'd like to include, such as plants, rocks, or gravel. A quarry or wholesale provider can give you a quote for different volumes of gravel. It is wise to have a budget with some amount of flexibility (within reason), as unforeseen costs, such as delivery costs for rocks or sand, can materialize when crafting a garden. Therefore, plan to have some money left over after purchasing each of your elements. Doing this research will help you better understand your conditions and limitations, allowing you to have realistic expectations for what your garden can become.

After determining your budget, consider how much time and energy you are willing to invest in your garden's creation. Plainly put, the larger the garden, the longer it will take to complete. In addition to the time you spend creating it, you should also consider how much maintenance you want to do once it is established. Most maintenance necessary for a gravel garden must be done by hand, whether it involves weeding, picking up debris, or raking. For your garden to look its best—and fulfill its Zen roots and aesthetic—

these tasks should be done regularly. Realistically establishing how much time you can dedicate to your garden per week can help you decide on how large it should be.

No matter the amount of space you are working with, it is always a good idea to start your garden at a modest size and expand it as time passes and you learn more about your unique space. This will give you a chance to experience firsthand how much work and maintenance are necessary.

Your property's footprint may dictate that you have only a small area for your garden. Do not be intimidated by your lack of space; some incredible Zen gardens have been created on balconies and patios. Because the purpose of these gardens is to embody the essence of nature, their size is not nearly as important as the care and design you put into them. This essence can be scaled down as much as is necessary to adapt to your conditions without sacrificing efficacy.

In fact, Japan's gardeners have refined the art of making a garden in tiny spaces. The tsuboniwa, or courtyard garden, is a great example of how a serene and meditative space can be created in a small area. Many Zen gardens have successfully been created in the size of tsuboniwa. If your circumstances are similar, you'll find a sample design for a small space at the end of this chapter (here).

Gardens of different sizes may use slightly different design techniques to achieve pleasant results. A small garden can remain very simple and still fulfill its purpose. For example, you may choose one element—such as a rock, a small tree, or a water feature—to be the focal point of your garden. Every other item you add can help balance your composition from your chosen vantage point.

You can follow the same principle for a medium-size garden, although you may want to use two focal points instead of one to better suit your space. You may, for example, let a tree and a rock dominate your composition, and arrange them in a way in which they balance each other as well as your garden. Other elements can be added to bring poise between these focal points without distracting the viewer.

An important consideration when working with a small or medium garden is the size of the rocks and plants you bring into it. Make sure that any element added to your garden is appropriate in scale so it fits harmoniously within your space. Research your chosen plants' size at maturity to make sure they will not outgrow their surroundings. Working with dwarf or slow-growing plants can be favorable in smaller spaces, and a bonsai technique may come in handy to keep your plant size manageable and in balanced proportion to the overall garden design.

A large space may provide you with a multitude of different perspectives from which you can contemplate your garden as you move through it. Although balance is still important even in a vast space, you have a bit more leeway with the size of your elements, as it will be harder for them to outgrow that larger space. Alternatively, you may prefer a primarily empty space and decide to bring in only a few rocks and a large expanse of gravel, in the style of the Ryōan-ji Zen garden (here). A larger garden may be a smart option if you intend to include preexisting mature trees in your composition, as they will be easier to offset with more space and larger elements.

Because a guiding principle of Zen gardens is kanso, or simplicity, small, medium, or large gardens may include the same number of elements. Remember, beyond gravel and a few rocks, every element you add to your Zen garden is optional. If what attracts you the most to these meditative spaces is their minimalism, you may favor a larger garden to create more empty space to invite contemplation.

More important than the size of your garden is how your composition fits into your landscape as a whole. You garden should merge seamlessly with its environment. Therefore, when designing your garden, think about the size necessary for your garden to look its most harmonious with your land. If you do this successfully, it will appear as if there is no beginning and no end to your garden.

Shape

Although many notable shapes can be found within the Zen garden, the shape of the garden itself is often freeform. A few recurring garden shapes are popular, however. Many traditional Zen gardens, such as the one at the temple of Ryōan-ji (here), are rectangular. The L shape is another common model. Often enveloping the corner of a building, these L-shaped gardens go beyond what the eye can see from any one perspective. Their form gives them the ability to look like they go on indefinitely, embodying through this aspect the concept of yūgen, or subtle profundity. In addition to being linear, the contours in Zen gardens can be oval, and sometimes they feature unique shapes consisting of undulating lines. These oddly shaped gardens are sometimes a result of design but more often embody these formats to adapt to their respective landscapes.

Keeping this adaptability in mind, your most important asset in choosing the shape of your Zen garden is your ability to be flexible. Since your sea of gravel should be on a flat piece of land, notice where your garden is naturally flat, and allow the elevation to organically create the shape of your garden for you. If your land is completely flat, you have more creative freedom, but try to avoid a perfectly symmetrical rock garden shape, such as a circle or square.

Because the shape of a Zen garden is so often dictated by its environment, placing your garden on an oddly shaped lot doesn't have to be challenging. Whether your lot is rectangular, square, or triangular, the rule to follow to create a successful Zen garden is simple: Avoid symmetry. If your lot is perfectly symmetrical, ensure that your rock garden breaks this symmetry by having a curved or irregular contour. You can decide whether you'd like to have a wavy or linear garden based on the kind of landscape you wish to create. Generally, straight lines make your garden look more modern, while curved lines make your garden appear more natural and organic.

Although the contour of your Zen garden can be nebulous or unstructured, many shapes appear or are sometimes subtly hinted at. Often, these shapes honor or symbolize different parts of the Buddhist religion or Japanese culture. One such traditional shape is the double peninsula, where two mounds bleed into the karesansui, or pond, from its surrounding landscape. Another similar shape is a long, narrow bar that cuts into the gravel garden. This shape, called an Amanohashidate peninsula, pays tribute to Miyazu Bay, one of Japan's most revered landscapes.

THE SHAPE OF STONES

In addition to the island forms, the shapes of rocks and boulders are of utmost importance in traditional gardens. Rocks that resemble boats, cranes, turtles, dragons, or other mythological deities are highly desirable, sought after, and often purchased for a considerable sum. In addition to these rare rocks, commonly shaped boulders are also mindfully chosen based on their form.

Each rock shape, whether unique or commonplace, is said to have a different purpose, something to consider when choosing the rocks to invite into your composition. A stone that is longer than it is wide and placed vertically is said to bring a feeling of excitement to your garden. On the other hand, a stone that is as wide as it is tall is reputed to bring a sense of relief and comfort to your space. Such a rock should be placed horizontally and buried at least halfway into the earth so it looks firmly anchored within the landscape. A smaller, wider stone is said to fill the garden with a sense of calm and tranquility.

THE TRIANGLE TECHNIQUE

Larger geometric shapes, like the asymmetrical triangle, can be used to help find the ideal placement of rocks, islands, and other elements in your Zen garden. When composing your design, using this triangle can help ensure your garden composition remains asymmetrical and balanced within Zen aesthetics.

To employ this technique, visualize a triangle with unequal sides being traced in the center of any three focal points (such as rocks, plants, trees, and so forth). No element should be placed in the center of the garden; in other words, do not place one of the corners of the triangle in the middle of the composition. This technique can be used on the vertical plane as well as the horizontal. You can utilize this design method when you are looking at your garden directly (this being the vertical plane) and when you are designing the plan of your garden and looking at it from above (this being the horizontal plane).

By using this technique, the elements of your garden will always be placed asymmetrically, ensuring that the concept of fukinsei is effortlessly reflected in your design. You can use this shape and principle to determine the placement of rocks, plants, and other large elements that draw the viewer's eye in the garden. You'll see this technique in action in some of the design samples provided at the end of this chapter (here).

Similar types of elements are often added in odd numbers in Zen gardens, which makes the triangle technique especially useful. You can use a similar method when positioning elements that come in pairs. Rather than visualizing a triangle between the elements, visualize a diagonal. As with the triangle technique, this method can be used in both the vertical and horizontal planes. Using this technique will ensure that depth is created among the elements and that you are avoiding perfect symmetry.

DISCOVERING YOUR ZONE

Plant hardiness zones are determined based on the climatic conditions and temperatures of a geographic location. When a plant is "hardy" in a specific zone, it can withstand the coldest temperature in that location. Knowing your specific growing zone will help you easily select plants that are more likely to thrive in your garden and avoid planting ones that might not flourish as readily. See Resources for more on discovering your zone along with a resource on how to convert these zones if you live outside the United States.

Elements

As you've learned, successful Japanese gardens embody the essence of their natural environment. For this reason, it's preferable to use plants and rocks native to your surroundings. By using naturally occurring material and putting time and intention into choosing these elements, your garden will reflect the principle of shizen, or naturalness with intention.

The more closely you get to know your environment, the more you can condense and honor it in your garden. Better yet, if there is one in your area, visit a botanical garden featuring a Zen landscape. Whether going to a garden or a nearby park, notice the colors, textures, and materials of the rocks you see in these locations. Take note of plants you see that are naturally thriving. Observe the conditions where they appear, such as how much sunlight and shade they receive. From these excursions, you will gain a better understanding of your habitat, as well as inspiration to potentially explore in your own garden.

Once you have gained a thorough understanding of both your general environment and your specific location, start brainstorming the elements you think will do well in your garden. Selecting these elements should be done consciously and deliberately. First, determine your budget. Once you know how much money you are willing to spend, think about the elements that appeal to you. What is most important for you to include? What could be a secondary feature in your own unique perspective? As you gather a list of elements you think will work well in your garden, remember that in addition to liking your elements individually, you should choose them based on their ability to work well together. They should look at home in your garden's location and harmoniously merge with your existing landscape.

You may have noticed native plants you think will be a good fit for your garden, or you may decide to use some of the plants mentioned in chapter 3 (here). Before visiting your local nursery or garden supply store to acquire them, take a moment to make sure your garden will be a good fit for them. First, if you do not know it already, determine the zone you live in to ensure the plants you are interested in will thrive in your climate. Second, pay attention to the specific conditions of the location of your garden. Observe the amount of sunlight, shade, and drainage your garden receives.

If you want to take it a step further, a pH meter, available at your local nursery, can read the pH of your soil, which can help you choose the most suitable plants to bring into your garden. Every plant prefers a soil of a different pH level, so knowing the pH level of your soil will ensure that you invite a plant into your garden that is more likely to prosper. Looking at plant books, researching your plants online, or inquiring at your nursery are ways to find out the preferred pH of your plants. Broadly speaking, if your soil has a pH of 7.0, it is neutral. Anything below a 7.0 is acidic and anything above is alkaline.

In addition to zones, other simple considerations can make sure your landscape is harmonious within its environment. The concept of shakkei, or borrowed scenery, can help you find elements that will look at home in your garden. This principle comes in handy if your garden sits on a larger piece of property. By using this principle, you take into account the existing scenery and use it as a natural backdrop, only incorporating elements that will complement this natural background.

In addition to selecting elements that look at home in your environment, you want to make sure your garden does not get too busy. One accessible yet simple way to do this is by acquiring one or two striking elements. These elements, which will more than likely be plants or rocks, must be visually interesting because they will act as the focal point of your composition. Every other element can be added to balance the rest of your garden. As mentioned in previous sections, the size of these elements should be thoroughly considered. The smaller your garden, the less space you will have to utilize perspective in order to balance elements. So, the smaller your garden, the more attention you should pay to the size of your elements to make sure they offset one another in a suitable, organic way.

With your list of potential elements on hand, check to see if they are available at your local nursery. Wholesale nurseries often carry elements that may be uncommon or harder to find.

Once you have compiled your list of available elements, construct a vision board of your garden. Take a picture of the space in which you plan to establish your garden and collect pictures of the rocks, plants, and gravel you are considering. By assembling these images either on a screen (using a free resource such as Pinterest or Canva) or on paper, you'll be able to test out whether the colors and textures of the elements you have in mind work as harmoniously as you first imagined. Ideas sometimes work a lot better in your head than in practice, and utilizing a vision board will allow you to see your ideas come together. This way, you can test them out without facing any consequences.

As you move forward acquiring your elements, keep the concept of kanso (simplicity) in mind. One common saying asserts that a Zen garden is complete when nothing additional can be removed from it. As always, what matters more than the actual elements you bring into your garden is their relationship to one another and to your garden as a whole. This interconnectedness is an important part of Zen philosophy, and it allows Zen gardens to fill whoever observes them with a sense of wonder.

Design

After selecting the location, size, shape, and elements of your garden and assembling your vision board, you will likely feel ready (and perhaps even impatient!) to start designing your Zen landscape. Follow these helpful instructions as you embark upon the design phase of your process.

1. Gather your visual aids. These include your vision board, to see how each of your elements works together, as well as pictures of gardens that inspire you. In addition to the designs provided in this book, gather pictures of some favorite Zen gardens. Spend time reflecting on your favorite parts of these landscapes and consider whether you can replicate these ideas and elements in your own garden and within whatever limitations exist in your landscape. With your references at hand, you will have a much easier time visualizing exactly what it is that you want out of your garden.

2. Acquire a plan of your space. You can do this in a few different ways. You may already have a blueprint of your house and yard, which you can copy and print to help you draw a design. If you do not already have this plan, you may acquire a bird's-eye view of your yard by using a service such as Google Earth, typing in your address, and printing a satellite photo of your land. A less high-

tech option is to measure out and draw a plan of your yard by hand. This may be a better option if you are working with a small area, such as a patio or balcony, or small outdoor yard area. Using a tape measure, measure your space and replicate its scaled-down dimensions on paper (graph paper can be useful for this exercise).

3. Mark important land features. Draw on your plan any driveways, patios, areas covered with concrete, areas with poor drainage, areas with elevation—any part of your land you identify as having special conditions. In addition, mark the parts of your garden that receive full sunlight, partial shade, and complete shade. This will help you designate the optimal areas to plant your trees, shrubs, and ground covers.

4. Draw your design on tracing paper. Rather than drawing and erasing several design ideas on your plan, sketch your ideas on tracing paper. First, draw bubbles to designate the general placement of your elements. Then overlay an additional piece of tracing paper on top of it. Using your rough sketch and blueprint underneath, refine your design by drawing a closer approximation of the size and look of your elements. Draw over any design ideas that do not work on a new piece of tracing paper. Use this technique however many times is necessary until your drawing is complete. As you sketch your plan, remember that you should adapt your design to your environment rather than try to force your ideas onto a landscape that is unfit for them.

5. Try out your design using props. With your final design sketch in hand, try putting together a mockup of your design in your yard with stand-ins. Use sticks or stakes instead of trees, rope to line the outside of your gravel garden, and cardboard boxes or other light, movable objects in place of rocks. Make sure that plants are reachable with your hose or water source unless you plan to use a watering can. What worked well on paper may not be as harmonious in practice, so do not be afraid to make some changes

from what you had originally planned. Record your updated design on a new piece of tracing paper once you have refined your plan.

Repeat as necessary. Be patient with yourself in this process, as designing a 3D space, especially a Zen garden, is not easy. After all, you are not working from a blank canvas but rather from a piece of land with its own particular strengths, peculiarities, and limitations. In addition to factoring these constrictions into your design, you must also try to create a garden that blends with its surroundings. Because of this wide array of considerations, take your time with this process. Focus on the meditative joy of the process rather than on immediately achieving a perfect result.

As you are designing your garden, remember it is most important for you to create a space that you enjoy. Now, let's explore a series of design samples from successful Zen gardens with an array of different shapes, uses, and sizes. You may get inspired by them, study them to understand element placement, replicate parts of their design, or pull ideas to incorporate in your own garden.

SAMPLE DESIGN 1: A SERENE COURTYARD SPACE

This Zen garden appears in the form of a tsuboniwa, or courtyard garden. This compact garden is a great example of how a Zen garden can fit exquisitely into a small space. This design, or one similar to it, would be a great choice for a balcony or a patio. Its simplicity and lack of clutter infuse the space with serenity and calm.

This sample features two focal points, a water feature and a tree. The tree, placed where the black dot is shown, is on top of a small island of moss or a similar ground cover. The tree that overlooks most of the garden is planted on the island, although it could also conveniently be potted and still bring harmony to the garden. For the water feature, a tsukubai, another simple rock fountain, or a shishi odoshi could work quite well in this design.

Because this a viewing garden, the angle of the water basin is critical. Notice that the basin is slightly angled from the walls. This intentional position allows the viewer to never have the basin facing them completely, achieving a sense of depth by having the basin placed at an angle. The water element is placed slightly in front of the tree rather than beside it, using perspective to give this composition a sense of depth. Looking at this design, you can trace a diagonal line from the center of the basin to the trunk of the tree (symbolized by the black dot), illustrating the asymmetrical triangle technique discussed here.

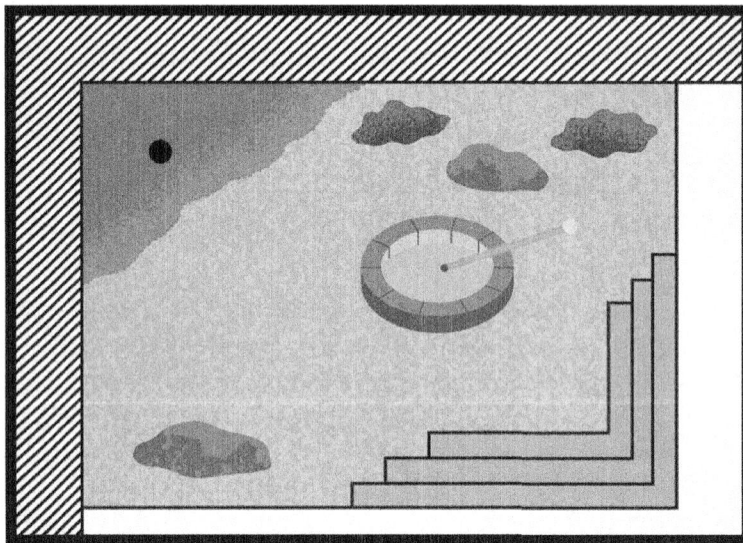

Gravel is usually used to represent water in Japanese gardens. Since this garden already features a water element, gravel is not used in this design. Rather, much of the ground is covered with small rocks. Depending on the texture and color preferred, different kinds of rocks can be used in this garden. Cobblestones and river stones, being smooth and rounded, will give the garden a more relaxing and calming atmosphere, while riprap stones and their sharp edges will make the garden feel more exciting and dynamic.

In addition to the rocks, water, and tree, a few plants adorn the water basin. These small plants further bring texture and balance to the composition by contrasting with the expanse of rocks. Just like the tree, these plants could easily be potted for convenience.

SAMPLE DESIGN 2: A CALMING ROCK RETREAT

This small, relatively narrow garden features an ideal design to place on the side of a house, between two walls, or between a wall and a fence. Such a garden can embellish the parts of your land that may be less aesthetically appealing and also hide elements such as drainage pipes, water heater valves, or similar necessary but less attractive house features. Because it features only one corner evergreen plant, this simple garden is extremely low maintenance. Incorporating this design in your garden is a way to give attention to and beautify parts of your property that are hidden or overlooked.

This garden features three large boulders, gravel, and a few small shrubs. It also features a few uncut flagstones that lead the viewer from the house to the side garden. Because of its simplicity and lack of clutter, this garden design enlarges its narrow space while imbuing it with a serene atmosphere. Although they are made of the same material, the boulders are of different shapes and sizes to harmoniously contrast with one another. Furthermore, you can see on this horizontal plane that they form a triangle with unequal sides. Although these rocks dominate this design, there is enough space to walk through the garden, preserving the landscape's practical and utilitarian nature.

Because the gravel within this design is meant not to be raked but rather walked on, larger gravel is preferable to smaller-grade gravel. Its color can be determined by finding a shade that complements the color of the boulders and the wall/fence. In addition to the single shrub in the dry garden (which is purposefully placed next to the wall of the house to hide an undesirable feature), a few select plants adorn its entrance. The Japanese holly (here) and the Japanese yew (here) would work well in this design.

In a side garden such as this, bamboo fences may come in handy. Such fences can be placed along unattractive walls or used as separators to create more privacy between your side and back gardens while complementing the elements in your side garden. This simple garden exemplifies many of the Zen aesthetics principles, most notably simplicity (kanso), asymmetry (fukinsei), tranquility (seijaku), and naturalness (shizen).

SAMPLE DESIGN 3: AN ENCLOSED CONTEMPLATION

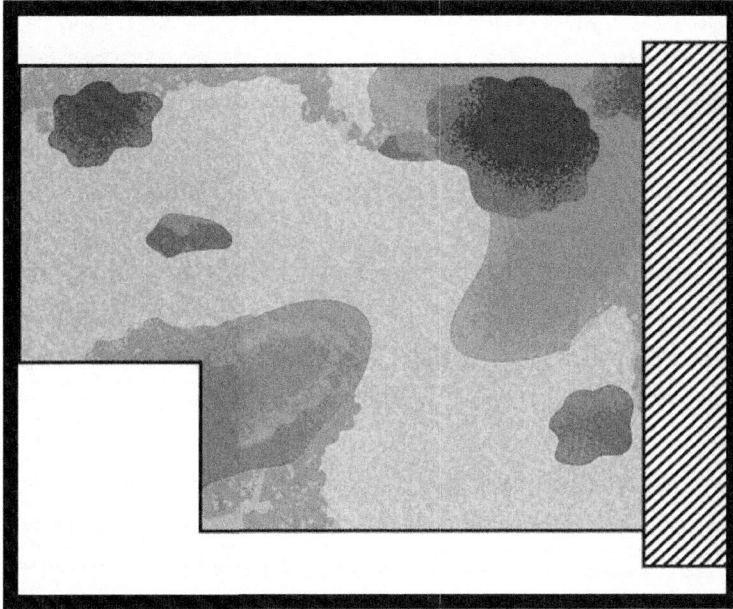

This L-shaped garden is meant to be viewed from several perspectives, from each window of the building it envelops. Serving as a viewing garden, this Zen landscape features the island design of the "double peninsula," a shape that appears in many traditional Japanese gardens. It features two boulders in a wide expanse of gravel, which can be raked to simulate the movement of water, and a few plants. On the right side of the garden, a mature tree dominates a mound of moss. The diagonal placement of the tree from the boulder helps balance the composition. Four other plants are distributed mindfully throughout this garden. Given their smaller mature sizes, they can be shrubs or small trees, or contained bamboo. From this overhead view, you can see they are placed asymmetrically on the horizontal plane, as the three shrubs form a triangle with unequal sides.

This garden offers an environment where moss can thrive. The tree, the large boulder, and the fences/walls that surround the garden provide the shade it needs to flourish. If you prefer a ground cover to moss, creeping thyme or mondo grass would work well on this garden's islands.

To add texture, the moss islands and one of the fences/walls are bordered by a hedge of rocks larger than gravel but smaller than boulders. These stones can be cobblestones, Mexican beach pebbles, river rocks, or a mix.

There are only three focal points in this garden, although from one perspective, the viewer can see only two at a time. Because the tree and boulder on the right side are close to each other, they should be of different heights to maintain asymmetry and balance within the composition.

From the other viewing point, thanks to their careful positioning, the two boulders are far enough away from each other that perspective can create a similar sense of harmony within the composition even if the boulders are of similar sizes. From the viewer's perspective on the left side of the garden, the two boulders will not be the same height. From both of its viewing perspectives, the expanse of gravel extends beyond what the eye can see, steeping the garden in a sense of mystery and vastness.

SAMPLE DESIGN 4: A QUIET STREAM OF STONE

This L-shaped garden is slightly larger than the previous design. Offering a pathway for the viewer to walk through, this garden is meant to be interacted with and admired from many different perspectives.

It features three mature trees, three boulders, and a few select shrubs. A dry creek of gravel runs through the entirety of the garden and is interrupted once by the pathway. This angular pathway features light-colored, square-cut flagstones or pavers contrasted against a darker Mexican pebble or river rock background. These darker, smaller rocks are lined with pavers the same color and material as the square stones. The wavy lines of the dry creek and the angular lines of the pathway contrast and balance each other beautifully.

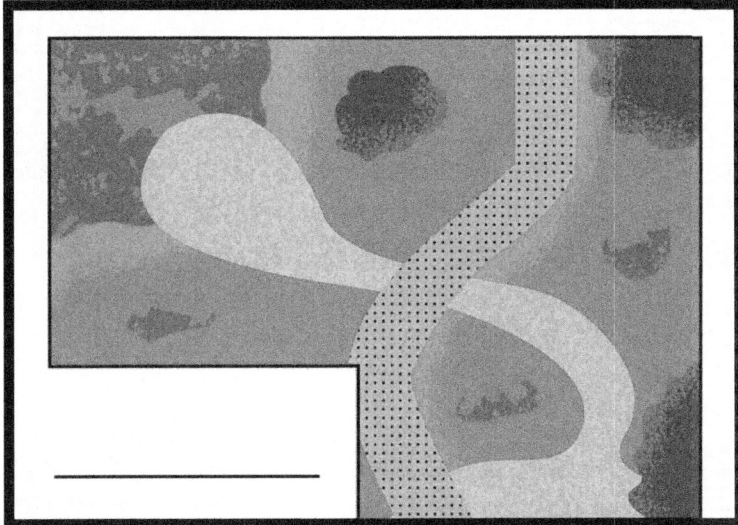

A dry creek like this one can be formed of gravel or of a combination of gravel and slightly larger rocks (such as river rocks and cobblestones) if you prefer more texture and nuance. In this sample, it begins on the side of the garden where the pathway starts and ends on the other side of the garden. The width of the gravel stream is not consistent; it begins in a wide pool, then winds around and runs in a thin stream between the mounds, and ends in a pond that can be admired from the pathway. To make this gravel pond even more interesting, it features a boulder and tree situated near its edge. The tree and boulder are of different heights, and their colors, sizes, scale, and placement contrast with those of each other as well as with the gravel and mounds or hills they dominate.

As opposed to the Enclosed Contemplation garden, this garden consists primarily of hills with a small creek of gravel running through them. Moss is a beautiful cover for these mounds or hills, but a different ground cover, such as Irish moss or baby's tears, can also be an elegant contrast to the dry creek and the pathway.

This garden demonstrates how a medium-size garden nestled between fences or buildings can feature an interesting and multifaceted landscape. It evokes the refreshing feeling of running water without having an actual water feature present and offers its viewer many different angles from which to observe, stroll, meditate, and reflect.

This garden also perfectly exemplifies how you can adapt your garden to the landscape that is already present instead of modifying it. Rather than trying to hide or remove mounds in your garden to create a flat karesansui, you can utilize them as hills, as in this design, and run a refreshing dry creek through them.

SAMPLE DESIGN 5: WHERE EVERY PATH LEADS TO ZEN

This larger and more elaborate garden features many interesting design elements, some of which were reviewed in previous sections. It juxtaposes a pond with a karesansui, and incorporates many pathways for the viewer to walk through and enjoy the garden from a variety of perspectives. (Note that this more advanced design sample is intended to inspire those who may dream of someday having a pond or those who already have a pond on their property.)

Within this garden, you'll see two traditional types of Japanese pathways: a shiki ishi–style pathway (a linear pathway made of regular paving slabs), which runs along the house, and a tobi-ishi pathway that runs through the garden. Tobi-ishi translates to "flying stones" and refers to an irregular pathway formed by natural, uneven stones.

In addition to the pathways, the garden features a few stone bridges that cross both the pond and the dry landscape. On the lower-right side of the plan, a rectangular rock space could be added next to the rock garden, creating a dedicated spot set aside for the viewer to pause and enjoy the karesansui. If you want to include a sitting area, this would be the perfect place for a bench.

In this garden, the gravel is meant to be raked and observed rather than walked on. Therefore, the quality and size of the gravel should be chosen with care: The particle size should be consistent and one that will not be easily disturbed by weather and wind.

Notable in this garden are the uses of the traditional crane island and turtle island (here), which appear in the pond.

Many rocks are consciously placed within the rock garden and used to delineate it. Because this design sample encompasses a larger area, smaller details have been omitted to keep the plan uncluttered. These include the vegetation present in the garden. (This landscape contains many plants.) The islands feature low-growing shrubs as well as evergreen trees. In fact, the spaces that surround the pond and the dry garden are filled with many varieties of plants and trees, most of which were present before the construction of this garden and were thoughtfully integrated into the design.

In addition to incorporating existing mature plants in the design, this large garden also utilizes shakkei, or borrowed scenery, underscoring how the existing landscape was considered when designing this garden, which fits harmoniously into its surroundings.

CHAPTER FIVE

BUILDING YOUR GARDEN

In this chapter, we go over the necessary steps and tools for creating the garden plan you developed based on what you learned in chapter 4. These include learning how to prepare your space so it is optimally ready to welcome your garden design, as well as the techniques you'll use to implement your design: laying down landscape fabric, positioning rocks, and installing other features and finishing touches. Last, we explore ways to nurture and respect your garden as it becomes part of your everyday life.

Tools

To create your Zen garden, you will need a few tools. Some are very important, others may make your task easier but are not absolutely necessary, and a few are needed only when creating certain designs.

ESSENTIAL TOOLS

Garden rake: A toothed tool used to rake dirt and gravel. Choose a high-quality, durable rake that's comfortable to handle based on your height. Cost: $20 to $40

Landscape fabric: Fabric laid down over the ground to keep gravel clean and weed-free. Consider finding woven fabric of high quality for best results here. Cost: $50 to $100 (based on length and quality)

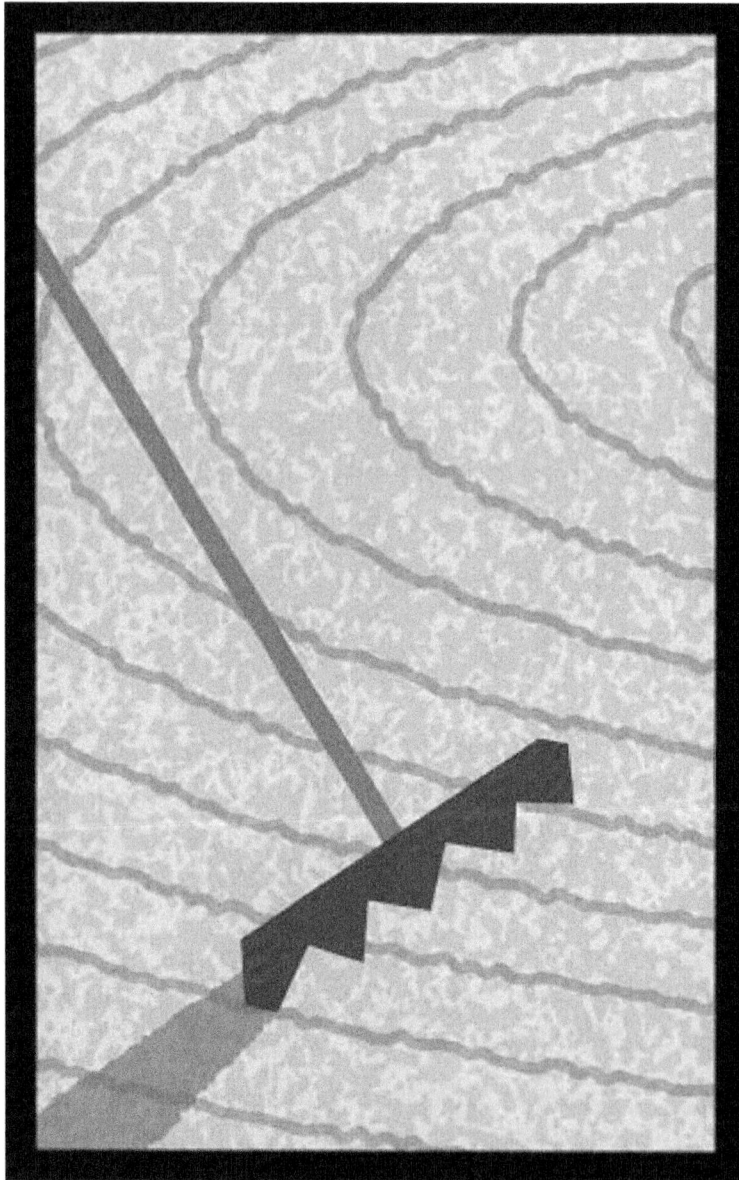

Landscape pins/staples: Used to secure landscape fabric to the ground. Opt for heavy duty staples that will not bend easily. Cost: $10 to $20 for a pack of 200

Level: A tool consisting of a tube filled with liquid and an air bubble used to determine evenness on the horizontal plane. For large areas, use a line level along with string and stakes; for smaller areas, use a 9- to 20-inch level. Cost: Line levels, less than $5; longer levels, $10 to $20

Nylon string: Strong string that can be used with a line level to check if the surface of the ground is flat and even. Using a noticeable color ensures you won't trip over it. Cost: $5 to $10

Shovel: A tool with a curved blade used for digging and moving materials. Choose one that is high-quality, durable, and a comfortable size to handle based on your height. Cost: $20 to $40

Tape measure: Used with line level to check how level the ground is. Cost: $5 to $10

Utility knife: Used to cut landscape fabric. Cost: $10 to $15

Wooden stakes: Used along with string and a line level; six inches is an appropriate size. Cost: $5 and less for a pack of 12. (Note: You may be able to find the stakes, line level, and string sold as a bundle for less than $10.)

NICE-TO-HAVE TOOLS

Gardening gloves: Used to protect your hands from cuts, scrapes, calluses, and any other injuries when constructing your garden. Cost: $5 to $15

Hand shovel/trowel: Used to dig smaller areas more precisely. Nice to have if you plan on putting in a lot of small plants. Cost: $5 to $10

Mallet: Used to tamp down soil or drive stakes into the ground. If you are using it only to drive down stakes, you can use a hammer in lieu of a mallet. Cost: $5 to $10

Soil pH meter: A great tool if you want to go the extra mile and test the conditions of your soil to better accommodate your plants. Cost: $10 to $20

Tamper: Used to tamp down soil. Cost: $30 to $50

Wheelbarrow: Used to move dirt. Necessary only if you plan on digging a lot of dirt to create your garden. Cost: $50 to $200 (depending on the size and material)

Zen garden rake (or landscaping rake): Although you can rake your gravel with a garden rake, a rake with more teeth may be beneficial if you are working with a wider area. Cost: $25 to $75

Preparing Your Space

With your tools and design in place, you are almost ready to start installing your garden! You may need to first prepare your space in a few different ways. Although not all of the following preparation steps may apply to your chosen location, please review them carefully. They are necessary to get your area ready so it will be an ideal space to accommodate your garden and allow it to thrive.

CLEARING THE LAND

The first thing to do is clear the land dedicated to your garden. Starting with a blank slate enables you to envision and execute your Zen garden design more easily. You may be working with a space such as a patio or balcony, where weeds do not need to be removed. In this case, take the time to deep clean your area to remove any debris, dust, clutter, or particles that can prevent you from realizing your garden design.

If you are working with a piece of land, start by removing any weeds, rocks, or plants not included in your design. Also remove any grass from where you intend to place your gravel garden. The area where you place your karesansui should be bare, as you should lay all of your elements, starting with the landscape fabric, directly on the dirt.

The landscape fabric, and then gravel, should be placed directly on the soil for several reasons. The first is that even the best landscape fabric cannot keep all weeds and grass from eventually poking through, so leaving grass underneath it makes for a lot more maintenance later as weeds grow through the gravel. The second is that the soil should be tamped and leveled to avoid future depressions in the garden (where water could pool), or incline (which could facilitate gravel getting washed away during the next storm). If you leave grass, you will have a hard time identifying irregularities in the landscape.

CHECK ON UNDERGROUND UTILITIES

If you plan to do any kind of digging, whether to plant trees and shrubs or to anchor rocks, first inquire about any underground utility lines that may be on site. In the United States, you can do so by dialing 811, the national "call-before-you-dig" hotline. This will put you in touch with representatives who can send somebody to come and mark your yard for underground utility lines so you will know where not to dig. Some utility lines are buried only a few inches under the surface of the ground, and hitting them while you are digging can be dangerous—and expensive to fix once damaged. This service is free, but it may take a few days for somebody to come out to assist you, so be patient.

MARKING

Once you have cleared your area and are aware of any underground utility lines, you can start marking your land using props to help you see where each element will go. Use rope to delineate the edge of your dry garden and stakes of various sizes to demonstrate where trees and shrubs will go. This step is similar to the last part of your planning process, except that you are now using your final, definitive garden plan. Be thoughtful and careful, and follow your garden plan as you initially envisioned it.

PREPARING THE GROUND AND LEVELING THE AREA

If you are making a dry garden on top of dirt, prepare the land before you lay gravel on it. Remove a couple of inches of dirt from where you plan on positioning your gravel garden. Then, make sure your area is leveled. One effective way to do this requires only a few stakes, string, and a line level.

Place the stakes on the outside edge of your garden. Then, attach a nylon string to each stake so that it runs across your garden. For example, in a rectangular garden, place a stake at each corner. Then, line the outside of the rectangle with string and make it cut across your space diagonally so that it forms an X.

After ensuring your string is tightly running through your garden from each stake, use your line level to make sure your string is level. If it is not, use your mallet to push the appropriate stakes down into the ground until your string is level.

Then, using your tape measure, measure the distance between the ground and your string in different areas. Rake any areas that are uneven until your ground is evenly flattened. Check the levels again and repeat this process until your entire surface is level. Once your soil is flat, tamp it down with a tamper, mallet, or your feet until it feels solid and compact.

CREATING YOUR BORDERS

With your soil level and compacted, you may now create the borders of your Zen garden. Depending on your preference and design, you may use cobblestones, riprap stones, pieces of flagstones, or whatever rocks you have chosen to create the borders of your dry landscape garden. Arrange a border that is at least one or two inches higher than your gravel bed to ensure that your gravel does not get displaced. Make sure each stone you use as a border is solidly anchored into the ground by tamping it down with a mallet if needed.

This step is not necessary if you intend to let the surrounding mounds of your garden be the natural perimeter of your dry landscape. For example, if you have a garden that has naturally occurring inclines, you can set your karesansui between them and let these slopes define the perimeter of the gravel garden.

With your space cleared, marked, and leveled, you are now ready to build your Zen garden.

Step 1: Lay Down Landscape Fabric

By now, you should have stable, solid, and level ground to accommodate your gravel garden. If you live in an area where the soil is naturally loose, and you find it does not feel solid even after you have tamped it down, add about two inches of sand on top of your dirt to make the ground more stable. This helps ensure the foundation for your rock garden is solid and sturdy. With that step completed, you can lay down your landscape fabric.

Landscape fabric helps control weeds and is an essential tool for making a gravel garden. If you plan to place your karesansui on top of dirt rather than concrete, putting a piece of landscape fabric down prevents your gravel from sinking into the dirt over time.

Additionally, it prevents your gravel from being in constant contact with the dirt, which results in cleaner gravel. Finally, it prevents most weeds from taking over your gravel garden.

Select a sturdy fabric of good quality, even if that means paying a bit more. Cheap landscape fabrics tear easily and can be frustrating and difficult to replace once your gravel is already laid on top of it.

There are two main kinds of landscape fabrics: woven and nonwoven. Nonwoven landscape fabric is usually made out of polypropylene or polyester. I recommend against using these, as they can sometimes suffocate the roots of your plants. Although they tend to be less durable than the woven varieties, they will still work if you do not intend to have plants in your gravel garden.

Alternatively, consider using a high-quality, woven landscape fabric, which is more durable, puncture resistant, and tear resistant. Woven landscape fabric has tiny holes that allow water and nutrients to seep through to the ground, making it an optimal choice for protection, aeration, and hydration if you plan to have plants in your gravel garden.

Once you have selected your landscape fabric, cut it to fit using a utility knife and lay it down on your chosen area. Cut the piece slightly longer than you need. If you are using woven fabric, note that the cut edge will fray, so fold the fabric so that the cut area is folded under. Pin this fold down with landscape pins. Once your fabric is securely pinned down on one side, pull it from the other side so it is taut over the ground. Pin the other edges down with landscape pins every few feet. The flatter and more tautly the fabric is pinned down, the less likely the rake will be to get caught in it once you rake your gravel.

Depending on the size of your garden, you may need to use several pieces of landscape fabric and juxtapose them to cover the entire area. If you do so, make sure you overlap each piece of fabric by about six inches so weeds do not grow up between them. Once again, be sure to pin the additional pieces of fabric down tautly, especially where they overlap with the first piece of fabric. This step may be time-consuming, but the more securely pinned down the landscape fabric is over the soil, the less maintenance and trouble you will have when raking your karesansui.

Step 2: Place Your Rocks

With your garden cleared and the landscape fabric secured, you can install your rocks. The rules for rock placement in traditional Zen gardens are quite numerous, and I encourage you to further research them if you are interested (for more on rock placement, consult the Sakuiteiki, in Resources. Although following all the traditional rules would be overwhelming, you can allow some of the essential ones, and the principles we've already explored, to guide you as you place your rocks. Following these rules will help your stone garden look natural and harmonious.

Stones should be set so they look stable, as if they had been in your garden for years. Avoid just dropping rocks arbitrarily on top of the land. A good rule of thumb is to submerge at least one third of your rock into the ground and to make sure the most aesthetically pleasant side remains visible. If you are setting a stone vertically, make sure your stone is buried at least as far as its widest dimension.

If you are placing your rocks in your gravel area, you first need to cut through your landscape fabric. Carve an X in the fabric with your utility knife and peel the fabric back to make space for your rock. Either cut off the extra fabric or fold it under. Next, dig your hole deep enough for you to place your boulder or rock at the depth guided by traditional rules. Place the rock into the hole. To stabilize the rock, fill the gap surrounding the fieldstone or boulder with gravel, sand, or dirt. Alternatively, if you plan to plant right next to your rock, use the appropriate kind of soil to best accommodate your plants.

After securing your fieldstones or boulders, begin placing your stepping-stones, if they are part of your design. If your design includes a tobi-ishi-style pathway (a meandering pathway of uneven rocks), dig a hole where each rock, fieldstone, or boulder will be placed. When you dig the holes, make sure that the ground at the bottom is as level as possible, and tamp it down so the stone can lie stably on top of it without wobbling.

If you are using slabs, consider working with stones that are at least three inches thick, as these heftier stones will better sustain foot traffic. Thinner stones may break when walked on and should be installed on a base of sand or gravel as opposed to bare ground.

If you are using fieldstones or boulders to form the pathway, bury them so their flat side faces up and can act as a stable step. With fieldstones or boulders used as stepping-stones, a good rule of thumb is to bury at least three-fourths of their surface. Once each stone is set and level, use sand, gravel, or the dirt you have dug up to fill in the empty space around your stone. Tamp each stone to further anchor it.

For these meandering, informal paths, lay the stones up to four inches apart. The farther apart the stones, the quicker the person walking on them will be invited to stroll through the space. The flat surface of these rocks can be anywhere from one to four inches off the ground. The higher the stone, the more carefully the walker will have to walk on them.

Above all, when crafting a pathway, remember that its primary purpose is functional. The pathway should therefore be safe, have a clear direction, and be enjoyable for you or your garden's visitors to walk on.

Step 3: Add Water Features and Decorative Elements

With your boulders and pathways in place, you are now ready to install other large elements in your garden. Feel free to skip this step if you do not plan to add a water feature or decorative element to your Zen garden.

If you have decided to incorporate a shishi odoshi into your yard and would like to build one on your own, see the Resources for instructional websites that show you how to DIY.

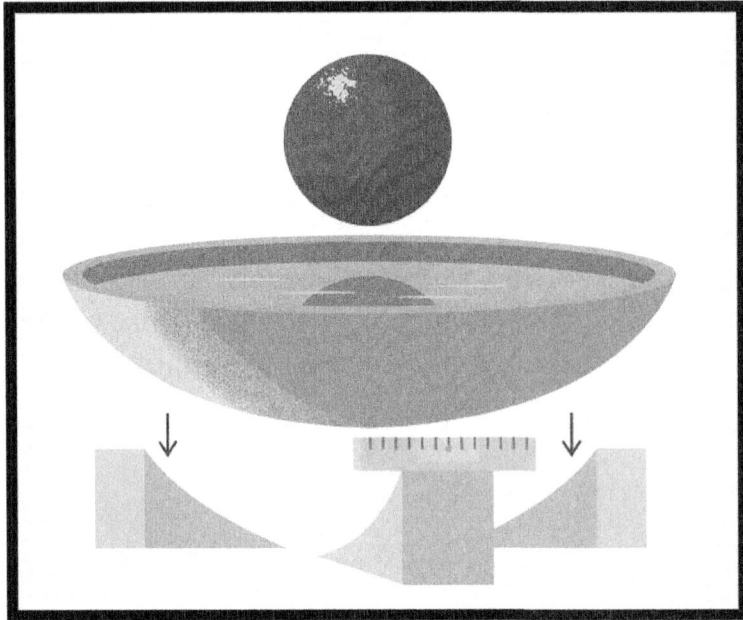

Although every fountain you buy may have different installation instructions, a few rules always apply whether you are installing a shishi odoshi, a store-bought fountain, or a water basin. Follow these steps with care and precision to ensure that the water flows evenly and that your water feature is not at risk of tipping over.

Unless you are placing your fountain on an already established concrete base, you must ensure that the ground is stable below the base of the fountain. Use a tamper or mallet to press down on the soil to make it solid and compact. If you install a water fountain on top of loose soil, it will become unstable and more easily knocked over.

Once your ground is compact, use a long level to make sure its surface is flat. If it is not, rake the soil to readjust it and tamp it down again. Repeat this process until the surface is perfectly level. If your fountain is made from several parts and needs to be installed in stages, make sure each part is level at every stage of the process. It is much easier to make small adjustments as you go than to level the entire fountain at the end. From a practical standpoint, if your fountain is not level, the water will not flow out of it evenly.

If your soil is very loose and you have a hard time compacting it, put a concrete base on top of your dirt to provide a stable base for your fountain. Compact the ground as much as possible, level it, and place your concrete slab on the ground. Check to ensure it is level, adjust by putting more dirt under the slab until it is flat, then tamp the concrete slab down with a mallet until it is stable.

Now that you have a stable and level base, and your fountain is assembled, install your water pump, following the instructions for your specific fountain. Add water to your fountain. If you are using a sun-powered water pump, your work is most likely done. If you have a traditional water pump, add water and plug the pump into a power source. Alternatively, add water to your water fountain at the very end of constructing your garden if you are concerned that dirt or debris may get in the water while you are finishing the installment of other features.

Other decorative elements may be set up similarly. Tamp and level your ground in the same way to install water basins and other decorative features to ensure they are stable and don't get knocked over.

Step 4: Plant Vegetation

It is generally a good idea to go from the largest plant to the smallest. Start off with your trees. Certain zoning laws restrict the growth of some trees because of their height, so make sure you do the necessary research in your area before planting them.

Trees and shrubs are planted in a similar manner. To plant either, dig a hole the size of the height of the container and twice its width. A hole that is wider than the container will allow room for the roots of the plant to spread out. If your plant's soil needs it, add compost, mulch, or other nutrients.

Once you have dug your hole and prepared your soil, put the tree, still in its container, in the hole to see if it's appropriately sized. The top of the root ball should be flush with or a few inches higher than the ground. Adjust by adding or removing dirt as needed. Remove the tree from the hole and spray water on the soil to dampen it.

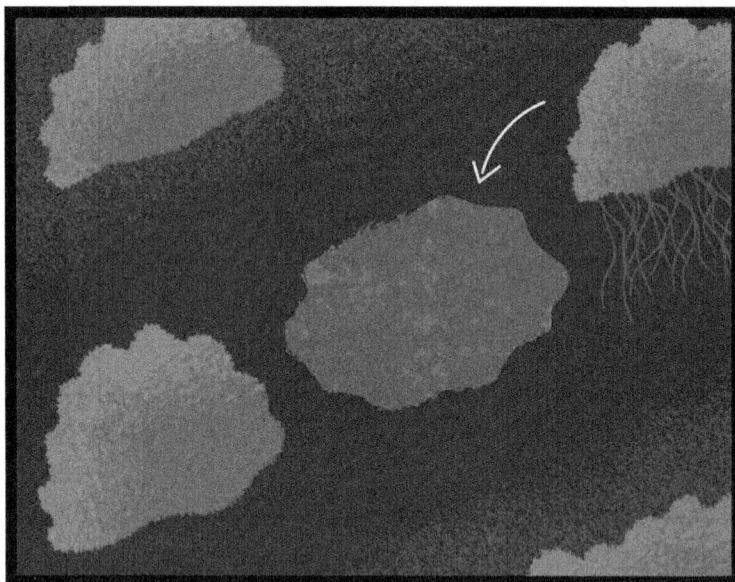

If you were to plant the tree without loosening its roots, they would likely remain in the shape of their container rather than expand in a more natural fashion. To mitigate this, cut the container off and, taking the tree by the root ball, gently loosen the roots with your hands.

Next, put the tree in the ground. Fill the surrounding area with dirt and gently tamp the soil to ensure the tree is stabilized. The ground should be compacted enough that the plant is stable but not extensively so, since roots will expand more easily in loose, loamy soil. Make sure the trunk is perpendicular to the ground. Prevent the top of your root ball from being lower than the ground level at all costs, as this may enable puddles to form at the base of your tree, which could lead to root rot. If you like, add a couple of inches of mulch over the base of the plant.

Mulching your plant will moderate the temperature of the roots and help them retain moisture and keep weeds away, and the mulch will break down into nutrients for your plants. Shredded dead leaves are a great alternative to mulch and may be found freely on your property. If you are planting your tree or shrub in the middle of your gravel, cut an X in the landscape fabric where you intend to place your plant, peel back the fabric, and follow the steps for planting.

Now that you have planted your trees and shrubs, plant your ground cover on your islands or between your stepping-stones. Prepare the soil by turning it over generously; in contrast to digging a hole, as you did for planting your shrub, you will want to turn over the entire bed where you will plant your ground cover. This way, the roots of each individual plant will have plenty of loose soil to expand into and will therefore grow more effectively.

At this point, an improvement can be added to your soil based on the preferences and needs of your plants. Read the requirements for your specific ground cover to determine how far apart to space them. Arrange them in a diamond pattern. Make sure they are on the same level as the ground. Once you are done planting, you can mulch or use shredded dead leaves to keep the roots insulated and damp.

Step 5: Add Gravel and Finishing Touches

You are almost done creating your garden! All you need to do now is add gravel and other finishing touches. Lay your gravel on top of your landscape fabric. Two to two-and-a-half inches of gravel is an appropriate depth, thick enough so bald spots are unlikely to appear, but not so thick that you will sink into it when you walk on it.

After you lay your gravel down, hose it or wet it down by hand to remove any dust particles that may have accumulated on it at the quarry or during transport. Flatten your gravel with a rake and refer to chapter 2 for different patterns to rake into it (here).

If your location contains too much incline to create a proper gravel garden, you can instead create a dry creek. Be mindful that in addition to being aesthetically pleasing, this dry creek will also likely redirect the flow of water in your yard. If your garden suffers from poor drainage, a dry creek is likely to improve its condition. Make sure, however, that the dry creek ends in an area of your property where water will be redirected to a well-draining area.

Place the creek strategically where the bed of gravel is always deeper than, or at least as deep as, its surrounding sides. To make a dry creek, first dig out 12 to 18 inches of dirt. Ensure that the dry creek is sloping downward. Once you are done digging, tamp the soil. Remove the dirt you have dug up with a wheelbarrow or a bucket.

Put landscape fabric over your tamped earth, following the same instructions as in step 1 (here), and pin the landscape fabric down tautly. Then place your rocks. You may use gravel, cobblestones, river rocks, or other pebbles. If you want your creek to look more natural, place larger rocks on the outer edges of the bank, keeping the gravel and smaller rocks in the center.

With your garden almost complete, start adding moss. When adding moss to your islands, test the pH of your soil if you can. Moss can be a bit tricky to propagate at first, and making sure your soil has the right pH for your specific species will help give it an environment where it will thrive.

Finally, take your moss and press it down firmly on the ground. In order for it to take in your soil, press it firmly onto the surface. Using pins or laying rocks on top of it can help keep it secure in the early stages of growth as your garden comes together.

Step 6: Nurture

Although your garden may look done, the final step is to nurture your plants while they get established. A plant being established means it is fully integrated into your landscape and is producing new growth. Trees will usually need less constant care, but they will need care for a longer period, perhaps even a year or two, depending on the species.

On the other hand, small shrubs and ground cover may need to be looked after for only a few months, but they will need care more often during that time. Among the most demanding of your garden's features, moss will need to be sprayed every day to keep it moist and make sure it propagates. Research the specific needs of each plant as it gets established, and adapt your care accordingly. Those needs may include regular watering, providing special care to protect them from extreme temperatures, or adding nutrients to the soil that surrounds them.

After placing your rocks, water features, plants, and gravel, your garden is now complete. Congratulations! Your space is now ready for you to mindfully maintain and enjoy.

CHAPTER SIX

ENJOYING AND MAINTAINING YOUR GARDEN

In this chapter, we discuss different ways you can enjoy your Zen garden. You will find three traditional Zen meditative practices and some less traditional ways to enjoy your garden while practicing contemplation. Next, you'll discover three important ways you can maintain your garden and see how to approach each of these as a meditative activity. Finally, you will learn about some common challenges that arise when you first learn to care for your garden and start a meditative practice, as well explore ways to mitigate them so you can be consistent both in maintaining your practice and your garden.

Using Your Garden

You now have a serene space to retreat to and enjoy. One great way to relish your Zen garden is to use it as a sanctuary in which to meditate. My own residency at a monastery was filled with several types of meditative practices, three of which you may find beneficial to incorporate into your routine.

These three silent activities—seated meditation (zazen), walking meditation (kinhin), and work meditation (samu)—are practiced daily at traditional Zen monasteries, and I hope they bring you the same joy, focus, and discipline they have for me and so many others. They are described in more detail in the section that follows.

You may already have a strong practice that you intend to deepen by working on your garden. In true Zen fashion, know that wherever you are is a good place to start. If this is your first time inviting a Zen or meditative practice into your life, however, I suggest you incorporate these activities into your routine slowly. Trying to meditate one hour a day if you've never meditated before can be daunting.

Rather than start a demanding routine that will be difficult to uphold, begin by setting aside a few minutes a day to practice. What is most important is to be consistent and to practice regularly. You may find that meditating even just three minutes every day is a good starting point, and you can increase your time once you feel that you have successfully incorporated this practice into your life. Once you feel ready, use your daily three-minute habit as a springboard to meditate for longer periods.

These traditional Zen practices are intended to open your awareness. They are wonderful tools for you to enjoy your garden, but you may find them too structured or formal to work for you at first. Having had incredible experiences practicing these Zen pursuits daily, I encourage you to try them for yourself, but I mostly encourage you to find what works for you and to enjoy your garden in that way. Meditation can take many different forms. Therefore, don't feel restricted to these practices as the only options for getting the most out of your garden.

Many contemplative and meditative activities can foster introspection and open your awareness. Writing, sketching, or making music may enable you to further enjoy your garden. You may love practicing yoga in the evening in front of your garden to wind down from the day, or to sip a cup of coffee or tea silently while watching the sunrise slowly change the hues of your Zen space. Your favorite way to appreciate your garden may be by observing it while having pleasant conversations with friends or family. There is no wrong way for you to derive pleasure from your garden, so do not feel restricted. Everybody's lives and needs are different, so explore different options and see what works best for you.

Finally, you should not feel like you need to do something in order to properly take joy in your garden. You may simply go to your garden and observe it. Pay attention to how the microcosm you have created is slowly changing, day after day. Notice how it interacts with the rest of your space. You created this garden from scratch and infused it with your hard work, mindful design, and attentive care. You may just find that the best way to enjoy your garden is simply to be in it, with no expectations for what you must gain, do, or feel from this experience.

PRACTICE 1: ZAZEN—SEATED MEDITATION

Zazen is simple to practice. Sit in a comfortable position and start silently counting your breaths: Count each long exhalation from 1 to 10; then start over at 1. If your mind starts wandering as you are counting, without judgment, start back over at 1.

If you have a meditation cushion or a yoga block, sit on the ground facing your Zen garden. You can sit cross-legged, kneeling, or, if you are flexible enough, with one or both feet on the opposite thigh (half- or full lotus position).

To sit with less discomfort for a longer period, make sure your knees are always positioned below your hips and you are seated on the very front part of your block or cushion. For most people, the higher you sit, the less strain will be put on your body. If sitting on the ground is too uncomfortable, sit in a chair or whatever you can sit in comfortably.

Straighten your spine so your abdomen is expanded, ensuring you can take deep, diaphragmatic breaths. Once you are comfortably seated, I recommend you set a timer for a specific amount of time rather than meditate until you don't feel like it anymore.

Once you are settled in a position, soften your gaze and start by observing your breath. When thoughts naturally arise, notice them, let them pass through you with no judgment, and gently bring your focus back to your breath.

PRACTICE 2: KINHIN—WALKING MEDITATION

Walking meditation is a great practice to synchronize your mind with your body. For those with the most active minds and busiest lives, sitting still for zazen can be difficult at first. The practice of kinhin is a good alternative for those who have a hard time keeping still. You do not need to have a large space to take part in this practice. Some of the areas in which I have practiced with a group were small, yet we still took part in this walking meditation by circling the edge of the room.

As opposed to walking with a set goal, the practice of kinhin does not worry about a destination. Walking several times in the same small square around your garden is a perfectly appropriate way to take part in this practice.

As you walk, bring your awareness to your footsteps and to your breath. Soften your gaze. Notice how the rhythm of your breath changes as you move through your space, and pay attention to the sensations that naturally arise in your body. Finally, be mindful of your steps and quiet them, so that your presence is as unobtrusive as possible. Most important: be with your footsteps.

PRACTICE 3: SAMU—WORK MEDITATION

Like walking meditation, samu is a great meditative alternative for those who have a hard time sitting still. Not only does this practice allow you to synchronize your body with your mind, it also allows you to practice full concentration on your action, and therefore it anchors you in the present moment while enabling you to take care of your garden.

The practices of weeding, watering, and raking are three ways you can partake in samu in your garden, and they are described in detail below. They are merely examples of work meditation, however; planning and building your garden can also be samu if you give yourself over to them fully. Any task can become a form of work meditation.

For a work task to become samu, you must fully engage with your activity. Watch your breath and let go of any creeping thought not related to the task in which you are involved. Give your full attention to your actions and as much energy and care to your activity as possible. Each time your mind wanders, bring it back to your activity. Be with your actions.

Garden Maintenance

Although a Zen garden does not require as much maintenance as a flower or vegetable garden, it still requires continued care to look its best. The more you can keep your space devoid of debris and unnecessary clutter, the clearer you mind will be when you practice meditation in the garden. If you have incorporated plants in your garden, watering is essential for them to survive—especially at first, while they get established. Depending on the size and location of your garden, the maintenance required may be minimal or it may be quite laborious. It may also include unforeseen tasks that do not include the three maintenance activities listed below.

Rather than view these tasks as chores, undertake them as part of your samu, your work meditation. In Rinzai Zen, the Zen tradition in which I train, work meditation is considered as important as seated meditation. Approach each of these three disciplines—weeding, watering, and raking—with reverence.

Engage in these activities fully, without rushing or being uncaring about what you are doing. If you run out of time, stop and pick up where you left off the next time you are available, rather than hurry through the process. Your consistent effort, hard work, and commitment to maintaining your space with care, precision, and full attention will reflect back to you in the harmony of your space.

Weeding, watering, and raking your garden can enable you to connect with your garden and, by extension, nature and the world around you. By requiring maintenance, your Zen garden invites you to fully exist, to care for it, and to be present in your actions.

CHANGING OR EXPANDING YOUR GARDEN

If you would like to change or expand your garden, begin by removing all that you no longer want to be there. Let go of dead or unsightly plants, discard rocks, and clear away weeds. If you are expanding your garden, you may also need to remove patches of grass. With your space cleared, you can start to envision what changes you would like. Measure how much space you have to work with, and realistically consider how much time, money, and maintenance you are willing to invest.

Once your intentions are clear, start planning the modifications to your garden. You may sketch out different possibilities to help you visualize your ideas, especially if you are working on expanding a large area. Although changing or expanding your garden is exciting, remember Zen gardens are minimalistic in nature. The space between your added elements is just as important as the elements themselves. You may want to meditate on the concept of yohaku no bi, the beauty of empty space, before expanding your garden. This can be a great exercise in mindfulness and diligence.

Brainstorm the elements you would like to add to your space. Before adding anything, consider the plants already living in your garden and how your changes may affect their well-being. Do not dig in a place that could hurt the roots of an existing tree or shrub, and be considerate of how new elements may prevent existing plants from receiving the right amount of sunlight. If you would like to introduce new plants, do the necessary research to make sure they will thrive in the environment you are creating for them and that they will not hinder the health of already-present vegetation. Temperature, light, humidity, and preferred soil acidity are all factors to consider when deciding on bringing a new plant into your garden. Working with native plants is preferable as they are more likely to effortlessly prosper in your climate. In addition, be especially conscientious of the size a plant will reach once it matures. Although your plant may fit in your composition at its young size, it might double or triple in size within the next few months, throwing your arrangement out of balance.

Once you have done the necessary research and planning, all there is left to do is source the necessary plants and material, modify your soil if necessary, and get to work. Whether you decide to add rocks, plants, or other elements to your garden, make sure each element you bring into your space has a deliberate home where it gives the rest of your garden a sense of harmony and balance. Your conscientiousness and attention to detail are in themselves a meditation and a wonderful way to delve further into your Zen practice. Your focused effort will shine through the thriving of your enhanced garden.

WEEDING

My residency at the Dai Bosatsu Zendo took place during the spring and summer. The monastery, in the Catskills region of New York State, is nestled between inhabited mountains, imbuing it with an otherworldly quality. Following the strict monastic schedule, we met every morning after a few hours of zazen and a silent breakfast so that samu tasks could be assigned to each resident. As the snow melted, the weeds grew by the thousands, conquering the open spaces of the 1,400-acre property. For days on end, it seemed, all residents were given the same task: weeding. For several hours each day, we crouched or sat on the ground and pulled each weed by hand, one by one, with our only tool a small gardening rake or a butter knife.

Whether spending hours removing weeds by hand is a tedious chore or a work practice depends on how you approach it. The harder and more laborious the task, the greater the challenge it can be to let go of your preconceived idea that it is unpleasant, and the more performing it can allow you to delve further into your practice. What a great opportunity to learn to let go of limiting and unnecessary thoughts!

When you pick weeds in your garden, do so mindfully, without rushing or letting your mind wander too far away from your activity. Please abstain from using any herbicide in your Zen garden. Pick each weed gently, but firmly enough to remove its roots, and compost it if you can. If you pull the weed by its root, the entire plant will be removed, and it will therefore not grow back as quickly.

The repetitive motion of pulling each weed from the ground can be incredibly soothing; find a natural rhythm at which your hands can work, and synchronize that rhythm with your breath. During this activity, let go of any thoughts that are unnecessary and fully concentrate on your activity and your breath. Do not be impatient; what matters is not the result of your effort but the process. As you earnestly clear the ground of unwanted weeds, you can also clear your mind of cluttering thoughts.

When you are done, your continued effort will be reflected in the openness of your garden and the renewed clarity of your mind. By removing the unwanted and unnecessary, you make space for all the good things you want to invite in.

WATERING

Depending on the kind of Zen garden you have created, watering may not be necessary. If you introduced plants into your space, however, you will need to water them, especially at first. (For more information on caring for plants as they get established, revisit step 6: Nurture.)

Watering may be an especially important task if you have plants in pots and/or plants in a partially covered area where they may not receive any rain. It can also be important in areas that receive little rain during the growing season. Watering as a work practice can be a great exercise in flexibility and, sometimes, finesse. You must learn to pay attention and adapt to weather conditions and the needs of your plants. Practice mindfulness by thoroughly researching the needs of each of your plants, as they likely all require different amounts of water. It may take practice to learn how to care for them individually. They may require different conditions to thrive.

As a rule of thumb, keep the roots of your plants from staying constantly wet. This is usually a problem only when growing plants in pots or gardening in soil with poor drainage. Wet roots lead to the roots rotting, one of the most common ways for plants to perish. To avoid this, make sure there is a hole at the bottom of your pot. Furthermore, pay close attention to how much water you give your plant.

When you are first assessing the amount of water each plant requires, check the soil with your finger. Maybe only the first inch of your soil is damp. In this case, you may give your plant more water. On the contrary, if you watered your plant so much that the soil remains wet, even after a few minutes, make sure the conditions of your plant allow for the soil to dry. Do not put your plant in a damp, cold environment where the soil will remain wet.

Researching the needs of your plants with care and your regular and consistent effort are great ways to practice samu. Day after day, you can use your awareness to see how your help is most needed in your garden and how to care for your plants accordingly.

RAKING

My heart still flutters when I remember the first time I was assigned to care for the Zen garden at Dai Bosatsu Zendo. I tried to not to let my excitement disrupt the serious atmosphere of the monastic setting. Once outside, the head monk taught me how to use the rake to trace a wave pattern on the gravel.

The design of the Zen garden was simple, but its shape was irregular. Most of it was oval-shaped, but one of its sides curved around the corner of the building, beyond what the eye could see from its main viewing point: the outside deck of the meditation hall. A single rock stood solemnly at the center of the garden. I was to rake circles around it until I reached the borders of the garden.

I drew my first circle with the edge of the rake right against the rock, so that the circle tightly enclosed the boulder. Then, planting the three innermost teeth of the rake into the three outer lines of my first circle, I used my previous pattern as a guide and slowly traced a new circle around my previous one. Slowly, the lines multiplied. The design I was tracing was reminiscent of the way the surface of water looks when a single drop falls into it. After a few hours of work, the waves had seized the entire garden, and I could not help but admire the gravel turned water by my rake.

Raking your garden is an incredible practice for unifying your body and mind with their surroundings. It requires full focus and precision to draw symmetrical lines. Before you start raking your yard, make sure your gravel is free of weeds and other debris. Next, rake your gravel so that it is as flat as possible. Wind and rain may cause the gravel to accumulate on one side. If you haven't done this in a while, preparing your gravel to be raked may take you as long, or longer, than the raking itself.

Although you may find it more tedious and less enjoyable, try to have no preference over raking or picking debris. Rather, view it all as one task that must be accomplished for you to care for your garden. Finally, give your full attention to your gravel as you give it the shape of water.

A WORD ABOUT PH

If your plants require a different acidity than your soil possesses, you can give them an optimal environment by amending your soil. If after testing the pH you discover you have alkaline soil and wish to make it more acidic, add compost, ground sulfur, or calcium sulfate. On the other hand, if you have an acidic soil and would like to make it more alkaline, you can add wood ash or ground limestone.

Acknowledging Common Challenges and Living with Your Garden

The challenges of creating and maintaining a Zen garden are the same as those that emerge when trying to maintain a Zen practice. Equipped with only enthusiasm and good intentions, you envision lavish possibilities for your garden and your practice. You dream of large expanses of perfectly raked gravel and of waking up at the crack of dawn every morning to care for your garden and meditate before work. These intentions are beautiful but sometimes not very realistic, especially when you are just starting.

For two seasons, I led such a life. I woke up before sunrise every day to practice zazen and samu, but even in a monastic setting, without the common distractions of the outside world, living this lifestyle was extremely difficult. Some days, I woke up exhausted. On those days, if I had not been absolutely certain that a monk would quickly notice my absence and firmly reprimand me for it, I most definitely would not have gotten out of bed.

118

You have courageously undertaken to create and maintain a Zen garden amid your other hobbies and responsibilities, but no monk will chastise you if you do not follow up on your plans. Living a life of high expectations is hard enough when there are consequences; it is even harder when no one is keeping you accountable but yourself.

Introducing a new practice or a new project into your life is difficult enough without having grand expectations for yourself and your garden. The challenges that manifest when caring for your garden and your practice come from these expectations you have created for yourself and your inability to meet them on a regular basis. When you practice Zen, you learn to let go of expectations, especially those you have created for yourself. Instead, you can fully accept where you are and what is possible for your garden. You can start small, both with your garden and your practice, and expand your commitment as time goes on and you feel more comfortable.

In addition to your own internal expectations, external challenges may come to disturb your garden. The wind may displace your gravel or uproot some of your plants. Deer or small animals may walk on your newly traced pattern and disturb your gentle waves, as they have so many times in the Zen garden of the monastery where I spent my residency. Nature, in short, may take its course. Rather than being upset, take this as yet another opportunity to delve into a very important Zen lesson: Everything changes. From these experiences, learn to let go of the tight grip you have over the illusion that you can change things that are out of your control.

Garden creation is a very special art form. When you build a garden, you give your attention, focus, and energy to a space, earnestly hoping that your creation will thrive. Past a certain point, however, your work is done, and there is only so much you can do to change the natural course of the evolution of your garden. You have given yourself fully to your task, and once you are finished, you have no choice but to let go and watch your garden transform on its own.

As you observe the passing seasons of your garden unfold, you are reminded to treat each moment with reverence. Your garden reminds you that each moment is fleeting, unique, and inimitably beautiful.

Printed in Great Britain
by Amazon

60979474R00078